NORTH ST. LOUIS CREATIVE FIELD GUIDE

Honoring the Land, Water, Ancestors, and Elders

4

The North St. Louis Creative Field Guide honors the land, plants, waters, and peoples of an area that many have called home for millenia. This place is located on the ancestral, traditional, and contemporary lands of the 𐓏𐒰𐓓𐒰𐓓𐒷 /Wahzhazhe/Osage Nation, Jíwere-Nút'achi/ Otoe-Missouria, Illinois Confederacy, Ogáxpa/Quapaw, Hocąk Wazijacira/Ho-Chunk, Myaamia/Miami, and many other tribes who have called this region of the Mississippi and Missouri Rivers confluence home. We also honor the legacy of the Mississippian culture that created home in Cahokia, the largest precolonial urban settlement in the present-day United States.

In addition to the Indigenous roots of this place, we also honor the important role that African Americans have in the past, present, and future of this area. The confluence of the Mississippi and Missouri Rivers has facilitated journeys for individual and family liberation from the vastness and brutality of the slave labor trade and segregation, which was concentrated in Missouri along these extensive rivers. North St. Louis's riverfront is home to Mary Meachum Freedom Crossing, a site on the Underground Railroad and surely where John and Mary Meachum's Floating Freedom School subverted a Missouri law in 1847 that forbade Black people from being educated by providing classes in the federal jurisdiction of the Mississippi River's open waters.

Like the nearby rivers, the lands of North St. Louis have also provided for African Americans. When the city was established in 1764, the area was designated as Grand Prairie Common Fields. The earliest Black residents there, both free and enslaved, took up farming.

By the early twentieth century, racial segregation laws, housing covenants, and redlining concentrated African Americans in the north part of the city. The *Field Guide* frequently explores The Ville neighborhood—originally named Elleardsville after Charles Elleard, a horticulturist who maintained a nature conservatory and greenhouses—which became a thriving community and home to the first African American schools west of the Mississippi, including Sumner High School and Colored School #8. Despite continual public divestment from neighborhoods in North St. Louis to this day, legacies of bonds between people and with the land persist.

The North St. Louis Creative Field Guide contributors encourage you to learn about the land and waters where you are, as well as the stories of the people who stewarded them. May your research be part of joining in traditions of caring for place and people.

Resources

Native Land Digital
native-land.ca

4theVille
4theville.org

Native American Food Sovereignty Alliance (NAFSA)
nativefoodalliance.org

Black Heritage Water Trail of St. Louis
slavery.wustl.edu/bhwt

Just as we appreciate the land and waters, we also express gratitude to all of the Indigenous Black and Indigenous farmers, gardeners, and stewards. In particular, the *North St. Louis Creative Field Guide* contributors pay respect to ancestors and elders, known and unknown, who have given shape to this project:

Gary Ambus
Leafy Anderson
Maya Angelou
Nathaniel Averyheart
Josephine Baker
Ella Baker
JW Bailey
James Baldwin
Fontella Bass
Black Artists' Group (BAG)
Alice Blair
Hamiet Bluiett
Williams Wells Broton
Gwendolyn Brooks
George Brown
Michael Brown
Patricia Brown
Clyde S. Cahill Jr.
George Washington Carver
Michael Castro
Elizabeth Catlett
Patricia Churchman
Amy Citchen (Haynes)
Anita Clay
Lucille Cliston
Bridget R. Cooks
Clement George Creamer
Lisa Croom
Julia Davis
Sharon Harvey Davis
Martin Delany
David Driskell
Joan and Ray Dezember
Joan Didion
Nita J. Dove
David Driskell
W. E. B. Du Bois
Katherine Dunham
Sr. Mary Antona Ebo
Ethel Mae Enoch Moore
Pete and Eva Ermigarat
Redd Foxx
Nikki Giovanni
Rosa Belle Grant
Grant Green
Rosie Greer
Dick Gregory
Galen Gritts
Fannie Lou Hamer
Evelyn Haynes
Duey Haynes
Eugene and Adletha Heffner
Leon Henderson
Milton Homes
Jeanette Hopson
Richard Hunt

Annie Isaac
Eartha Lee Johnson
Helen Malene Karasz
Mama Dora King
Oliver Lake
Shirley LeFlore
Sonny Liston
Elvira Lopez
Lolli Lopez
Tony Romero Lopez
Toussaint Louverture
Ethel Hedgeman Lyle
Jhonetta Malone
Tshepiso Matlapeng-Sani
Mary and John Meachum
Evelyn Miller (Haynes)
Pearl Miller
Mary Moton
Is'Mima Nebt'Kata
Ennis O'Neal Newman
Homer G. Phillips
Sylvia Plath
Mary Ellen Pleasant
Faith Ringgold
Paul Robeson
Marlene Schuman
Ntozake Shange
Charles "BoBo" Shaw
Nina Simone
Seitu James Smith
Alma Thomas
Harriet Tubman
Charles Henry Turner
Meredith Wilks
Patricia Ann Guthrie Williams
Douglas William
Alice Windom
Whitney M. Young

Foreword

Lisa Melandri

The North St. Louis Creative Field Guide emerges from a simple yet profound truth: what you feed grows. For over thirty years, Contemporary Art Museum St. Louis (CAM) has been a neighbor to significant North St. Louis communities. Over the past decade, we have cultivated relationships with the schools, organizations, and residents in our backyard. This publication represents far more than a collection of art that has come out of a community engagement project—it is an act of devotion to the people, places, and natural world of North St. Louis.

In 2024, a remarkable group of community members and artists came together to explore the deep connections between creativity, nature, and community well-being in North St. Louis. Through their commitment to paying attention—to the land, to one another, to the histories that shape this place—they have created something extraordinary. The *Field Guide* is both a testament to their vision and an invitation for others to join in similar collective actions.

My gratitude extends to CAM staff who stewarded this program and book, namely Director of Learning and Engagement Michelle Dezember and Community Access Manager Alexis Creamer. I am deeply appreciative of lead artists Dail Chambers and Juan William Chávez for again partnering with us to share their artistic and ecological practices. And I am truly humbled by the wonderful contributions of the dedicated working group members: AleXeana harlem, Cary Brown, Frankie Williams, Gabi Cole, Rev. LaQuindlyn Shanae, Ronda Smith Branch, and Tosha Phonix.

This project was enriched by community partners and sites, including A.C.R.E.S., Coahoma Orchards, the City of St. Louis's Planning and Urban Design Agency, Creative

Reaction Lab, Forest ReLeaf, and Northside Workshop. Furthermore, the *North St. Louis Creative Field Guide* was made possible by an award from the National Endowment for the Arts with additional support from the Regional Arts Commission of St. Louis.

It is a privilege to support this work and for CAM to be shaped by the input and creativity of our community partners. We hope the *Field Guide* offers new ways to see, appreciate, and care for North St. Louis, and that it inspires other forms of creative expression.

NORTH SAINT LOUIS

```
A N T O G E T H E R D A S A C R E D L L S
U B E A U T I F U L S E B L A C K O E A A
P N I M P A C T T H C E C A R E R F W N I
E B I E D R E A M A S P I I S M I E O D N
A U A T Y N D S P E D W E I R L A M O S T
C I N T Y N R S E O A T A O O C F M D T L
S L U T J E N B E C A R H R P I E I S E O
R D P O D E E F L O R A T L M L A S R W U
E I S A R V C H O K E B E R R Y E S E A I
L N E G I W C F W A T E R E H I M I A R S
L L A T M H T A O L D S S C O M O S D D O
E H A M O O H I O L R M R D M R U S E S I
T N C I T L E R I A U A N N E A N I R T M
Y C E S H E V G C R N G A H S S D P T R A
R H T S E E I R D O M L T E M P S P R E G
O I I I R L L O M O P R R Y M B R I E E I
T L H S S D L U M L O V E R I E F A E T N
S D C S Y E E N A N N R A A E R E N M S A
E R R I O R G D P P D F L G A R N K U C T
R E A P U B R H E A L I N G E Y C R E A I
U N R P N E E R E D B R I C K D E A S K O
T S E I G R A L A U G H T E R A A P U L N
C N W R P R T B L A C K B E R R Y N M A O
E A O I E Y E L L R B A B I E S S O C W P
T R L V O T R F E E S W O R L D R L S E E
I E F E P J V L C G A T S N E W E L I D A
H T E R L O Y I R M A R O O A N H A R I C
C A N U E L S E E D D C N R I I T F E S E
R E O P I J H E A L T H Y I I L A O N P G
A H C M M A N C E S T O R S N E F T S A R
D T A R E S I D E N T W E H O U S E L S O
L F R E S I L I E N T D E V E L O P I T W
```

To Pay Attention Is to Love: Notes on Creating and Using the North St. Louis Creative Field Guide

Michelle Dezember

Just north of St. Louis flows the confluence of the Mississippi and Missouri Rivers. For thousands of years, people have been drawn to this abundant area for its natural possibilities. However, modern colonization and development has often been in tension with the environment. In *Common Fields: An Environmental History of St. Louis*, historian Andrew Hurley challenges the "false dichotomy between the urban and the natural" by connecting nature and human settlements, from Cahokia (the largest precolonial city in what is now the United States and home to as many as twenty thousand people from 700 to 1400 A.D.) to our present-day metropolis.[1] This framing of the interdependence of cities and nature might help us mend human-made terrors: attempts to eradicate Indigenous people and culture, divestment of Black communities, social isolation and segregation, climate change, and patterns of dehumanization and ecological disconnection.

Humans thrive when we're connected to nature—and to one another. One of the best ways to understand the health of these connections is through our creative expressions. Creativity—like farming, gardening, or stewarding land—is an act of paying attention. It is often the evidence of how our minds are processing the world, and how we yearn to transform it. The *North St. Louis Creative Field Guide* is the culmination of a process that a small working group undertook between 2024 and 2025 as a community- and artist-led project that treats nature in North St. Louis as a way to build community, promote well-being, and foster pride in place.

Members of the working group live and work in North St. Louis, an area loosely defined as north of Forest Park Avenue, south of Calvary Cemetery & Mausoleum and

Bellefontaine Cemetery and Arboretum, west of the Mississippi River, and east of the border of St. Louis City. As these nature-forward names suggest, area residents have a long-standing bond with the environment. The original Indigenous residents—including the Missouria, Osage, Illinois Confederacy, and many others—hold a worldview grounded by a sense of harmony between human and natural life. To a degree, the colonial settlement of North St. Louis prioritized land cultivation. When the city was founded in 1764, the French colonists designated a system of "Common Fields" of narrow east-west strips based on medieval European forms of communal agriculture that predate the capitalist commodification of land (although this scheme was still based in dominating the environment). The largest true prairie of St. Louis, "La Grande Prairie," was an area on the north side of the city forming what is now roughly the Ville, Greater Ville, and Fairground neighborhoods.[2] Many nineteenth-century residents of North St. Louis, including white European emigrants, enslaved people of African descent, and free Black citizens, worked primarily as farmers.

In the twentieth century, the neighborhoods of North St. Louis underwent radical demographic and urban transformation, most notably in the case of The Ville. In the early 1900s, The Ville was one of the only neighborhoods where African Americans could own property, thus giving rise to a thriving Black community anchored by cultural leaders, businesses, and institutions—including the renowned Sumner High School, the first Black high school west of the Mississippi River. However, as population loss and systemic racism pulled resources away from the neighborhood, the number of residents decreased by nearly 40 percent by 1970, a trend that continues into the twenty-first century. As of the 2020 census, only a quarter

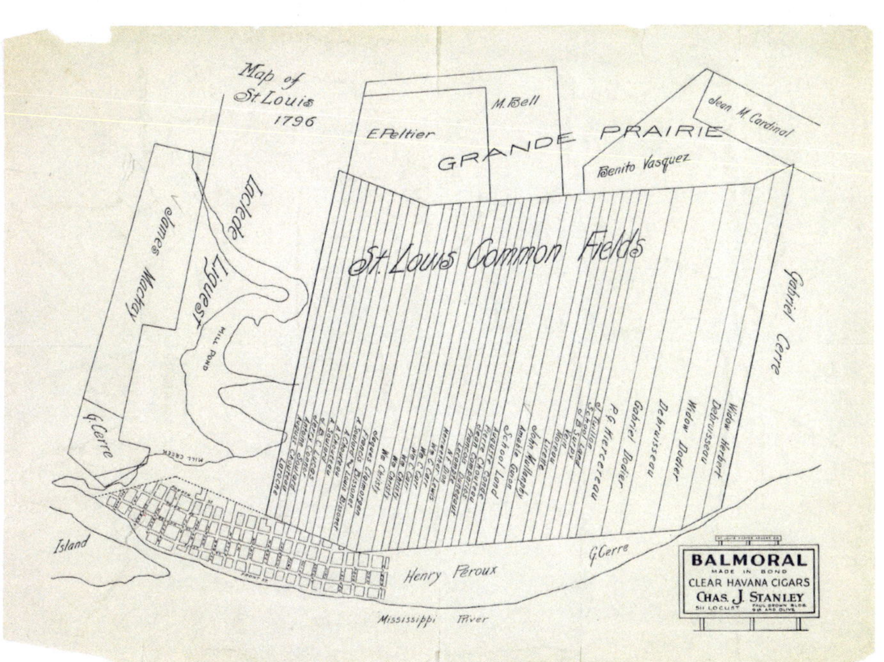

Map of St. Louis 1796
M. Bell
E. Peltier
GRANDE PRAIRIE
Jean M. Cardinal
Benito Vasquez
Laclede
James Mackay
Liguest
MILL POND
St. Louis Common Fields
Gabriel Cerre
Widow Herbert
Debrusseau
Widow Dodier
Debruisseau
Gabriel Dodier
School Land
John Mullanphy
G. Cerre
MILL CREEK
Island
Henry Peroux
G. Cerre
Mississippi River
BALMORAL
MADE IN BOND
CLEAR HAVANA CIGARS
CHAS. J. STANLEY
511 LOCUST
PAUL BROWN BLDG. 9th AND OLIVE

of the peak population remained. Despite divestment, negative stereotyping, and even a devastating EF3 tornado in May 2025, The Ville persists as culturally and ecologically significant thanks to its passionate community. Though this is just one trajectory—and each neighborhood in North St. Louis bears its unique set of histories—a different kind of "common field" of shared experiences extends across this area of the city.

The *North St. Louis Creative Field Guide* project started in summer 2024. In my role as Director of Learning and Engagement at CAM, along with my colleague Alexis Creamer, the Museum's Community Access Manager, we invited artists Dail Chambers and Juan William Chávez as thought partners to give shape to our intentions. Next we assembled a cohort of community members to join us: AleXeana harlem, Cary Brown, Frankie Williams, Gabi Cole, Rev. LaQuindlyn Shanae, Ronda Smith Branch, and Tosha Phonix. As a working group, we took several months to build community agreements and uplift individual capacity. To consider other efforts across the city, we hosted guests, including Andrea Godshalk, Elysia Russell, Jonathan Roper, Alexa Seda, and Mike Ziegler from the City of St. Louis's Planning and Urban Design Agency; Antionette Carroll of Creative Reaction Lab; and Rebecca Hankins and Kelly Hicks-Holloway from Forest ReLeaf. We also valued spending time in nature at spaces stewarded by members of our group: Coahoma Orchards in The Ville, Northside Workshop in Old North, and A.C.R.E.S. in Walnut Park. As our sessions came to a close, each member developed a project inspired by their experiences.

What follows in this book is a contribution from each group member. We followed a pedagogical model of gradual release, beginning with guided demonstration, followed by learning and testing, and ultimately arriving at each person taking self-directed action.[3] We hope that a similar process might unfold for you, dear reader, that you might take inspiration from the enclosed artworks, photographs, and texts.

We chose the framing device of a field guide because the format prioritizes readers being outside and paying attention to the environment. It is important to note that this book was never intended to be an exhaustive or authoritative inventory of efforts in North St. Louis. Rather, we focus on the perspectives of the members of the working group to exemplify the power of coming together in community as a way to hone our attention.

How to Use the Field Guide

The book is organized around the four seasons, which correspond with four elements of lead artist Dail Chambers's practice. You are encouraged to use your intuition and observational skills to move through the book in an organic, nonlinear way that best responds to what you need at any given moment.

We invite you to read this book before or while being outside. You can follow the prompts below to experience how different ways of being with nature can be a kind of meditation. A sketchbook—either one you find or make with scrap paper—can be a helpful companion for making sketches and notes of what you notice.

Sitting

Being in the field can be as simple as porch sitting, stargazing, or quietly observing from a park bench.

How does the air feel on my skin?

What different colors do I notice in the nature that surrounds me?

What do the sounds I hear tell me about life in this place at this moment?

What plants do I see? What stage of development are they in (seedling, blooming, decomposing)?

What insects and animals do I see?

How am I connected to these plants and animals?

Walking
If you feel comfortable, build on these prompts to explore movement through nature in the form of a gentle walk.

Buddhist monk, peace activist, writer, and teacher Thich Nhat Hanh provides guidance for a walking meditation:

> Be aware of the contact between your feet
> and the Earth.
> Walk as if you are kissing the Earth with your feet.
> We have caused a lot of damage to the Earth.
> Now it is time for us to take good care of her.[4]

What do I notice as I walk?

What did I feel called to walk toward (or away from)?

What don't I see in this environment? Has anything been removed or erased?

Gardening and Farming
Follow these prompts if you have access to nature that you are safe to tend to by gardening or farming.

What is familiar about these plants? What is unfamiliar?

What experience am I having as I work and/or play with these plants?

What kinds of actions feel the most enjoyable?

How do I feel different after this experience?

Where to Use the Field Guide

This book was developed specifically in and about nature in North St. Louis.

If you live in North St. Louis, go to the closest space where you can connect with nature. This could even be at home with a potted plant or any nature that immediately surrounds you.

If you live in another part of the area, appreciate one of the many public green spaces available in North St. Louis. This could be a park, a community or private garden or farm that posts an invitation for guests, or another urban green space, such as the greenery maintained by the Griot Museum of Black History.

If you live in another part of the world, take inspiration from one of the contributors here to do your own research on the community where you live. Maybe you can support North St. Louis from a distance financially or with words of encouragement.

Why Use the Field Guide

With so many narratives reducing North St. Louis to a headline or statistic, it is important to share community voices in creative formats. We believe this kind of storytelling has real power; as the adage goes, "what you feed grows." In 1982, Audre Lorde published *Zami: A New Spelling of My Name* as an experimental form of literature that combined autobiography, history, and myth in a new genre she identified as "biomythography."[5] Similarly, the *Field Guide* texts range in tone and style—historical, poetic, fieldwork, and speculative—while all being deeply personal. This blend of genres offers an opportunity to notice different dimensions and contemplate the possibilities of the natural and human creativity in North St. Louis.

Many acts of love and labor have made this book possible. I offer my gratitude to the working group contributors of this book and the process that created it; to Izaiah Johnson and Tyler Small for beautiful photography; to Graham Eng-Wilmot for not only being the best partner in every sense, but also for helping the group's truest intentions come through in words; and to Kevin McCoy for giving the book its visual form and identity. And, ultimately, my love goes to the people and place of North St. Louis: to pay attention is to love. May we commit to giving you both in the equal measures you deserve.

Notes

1.
Common Fields: An Environmental History of St. Louis, ed. Andrew Hurley (St. Louis: Missouri Historical Society Press, 1997).

2.
Walter A. Schroeder, "Presettlement Prairie of Missouri" (Missouri Department of Conservation, 1982).

3.
"Connect, Inspire & Collaborate: YES! Activities Facilitation Manual For Young Changemakers" (Santa Cruz, CA: YES!, 2010).

4.
Thich Nhat Hanh, Peace Is Every Step (New York: Bantam, 1990).

5.
Audre Lorde, *Zami: A New Spelling of My Name* (Watertown, MA: Persephone Press, 1982).

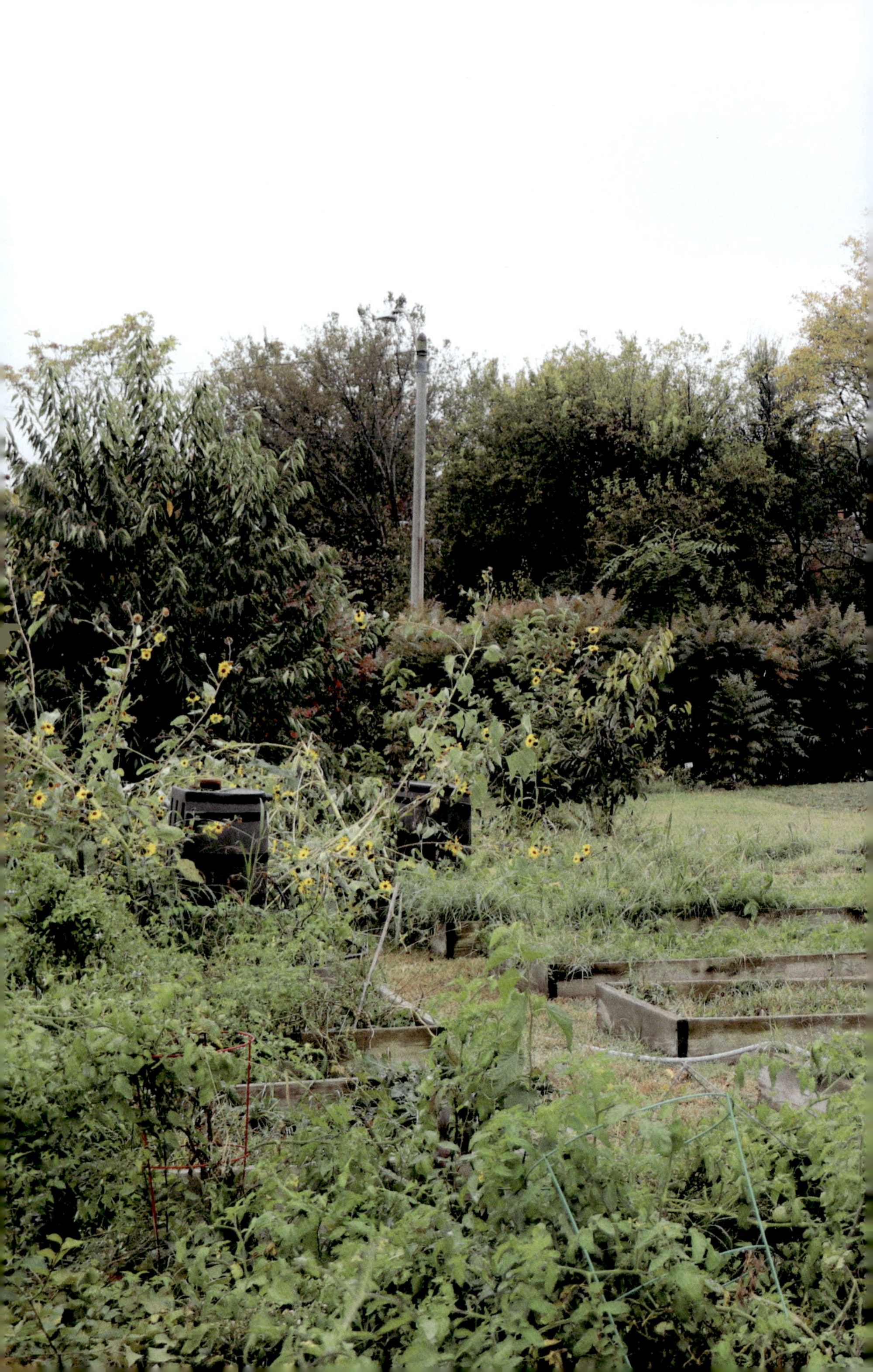

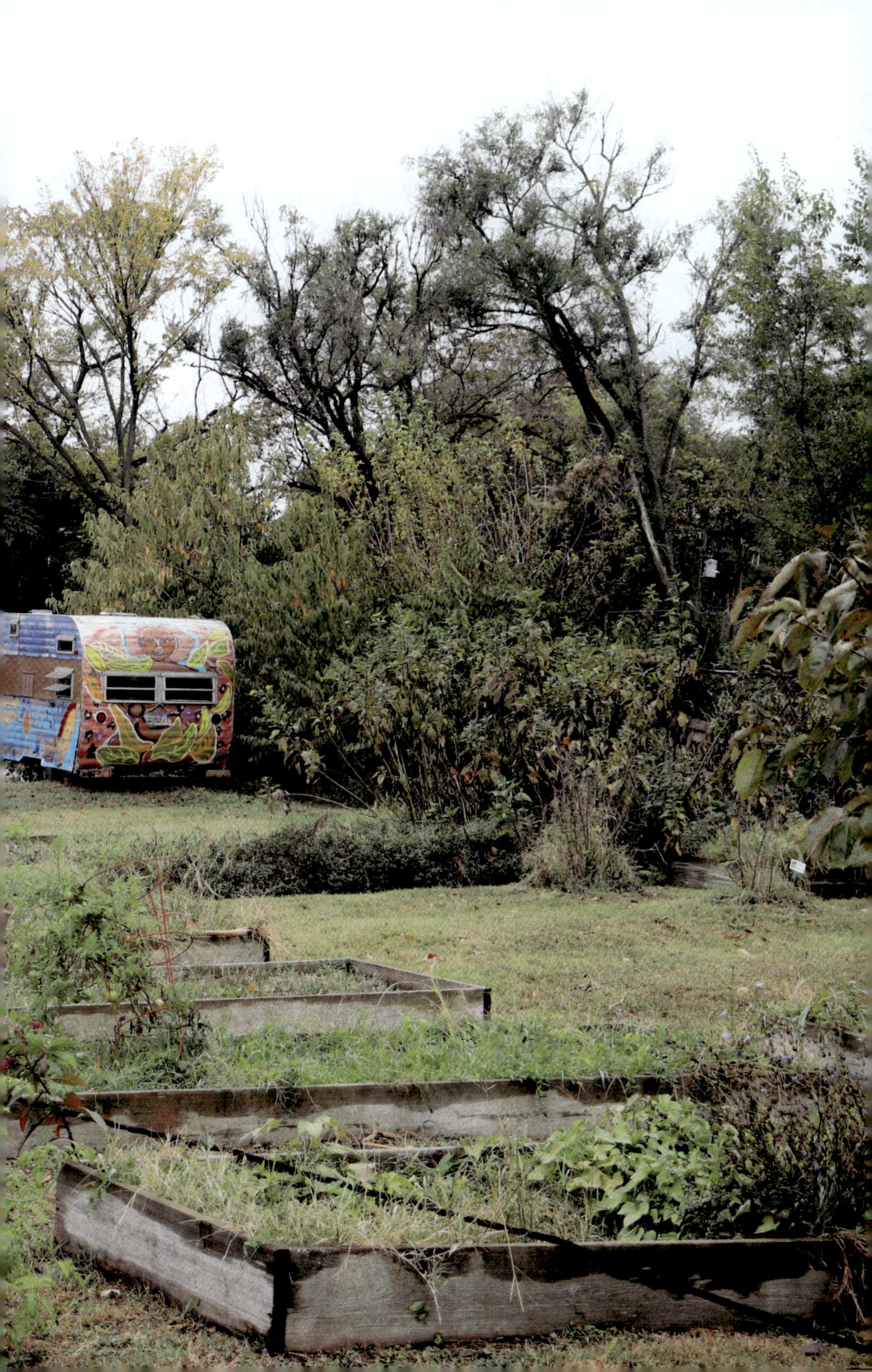

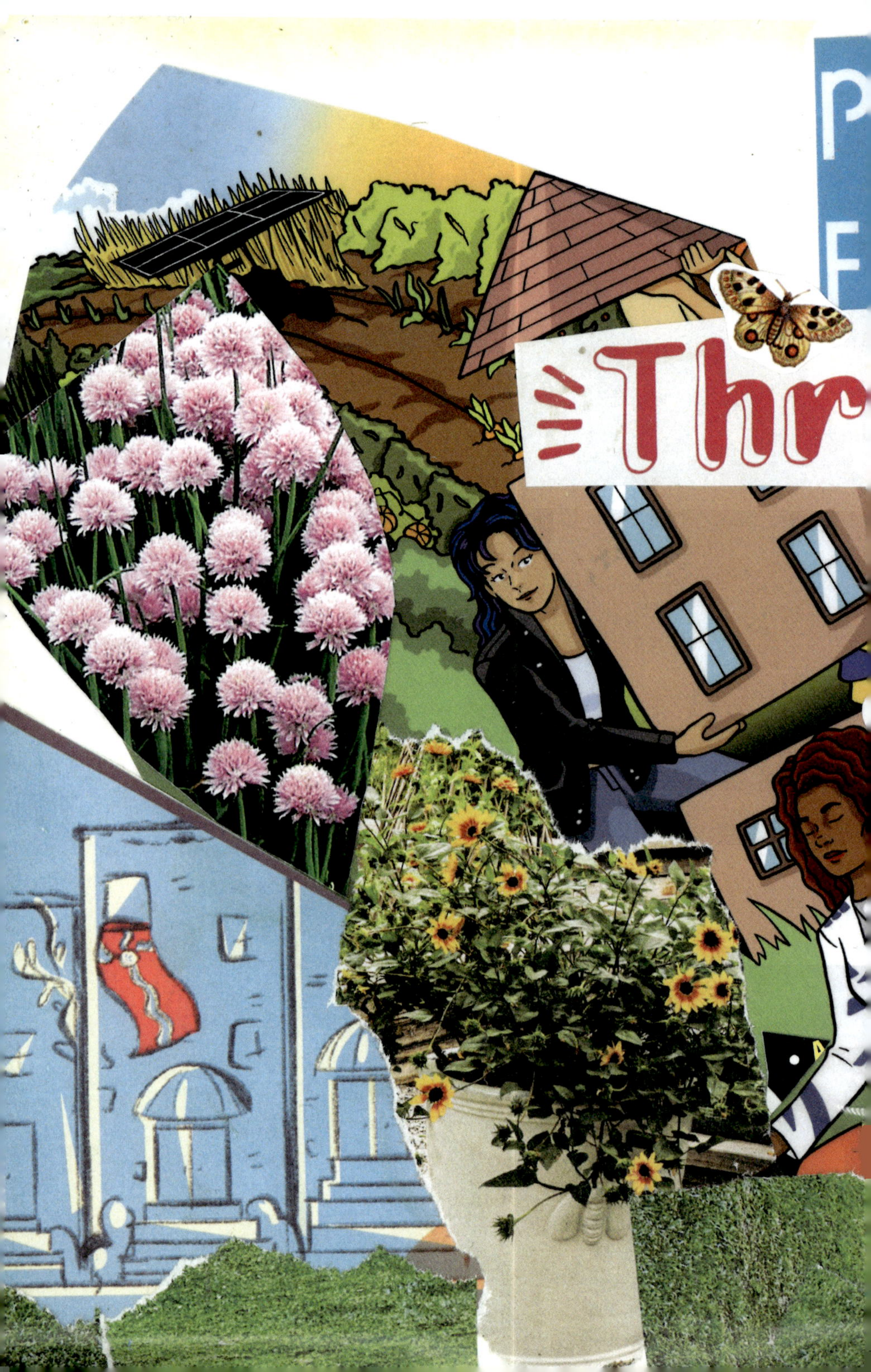
P
F
Thr

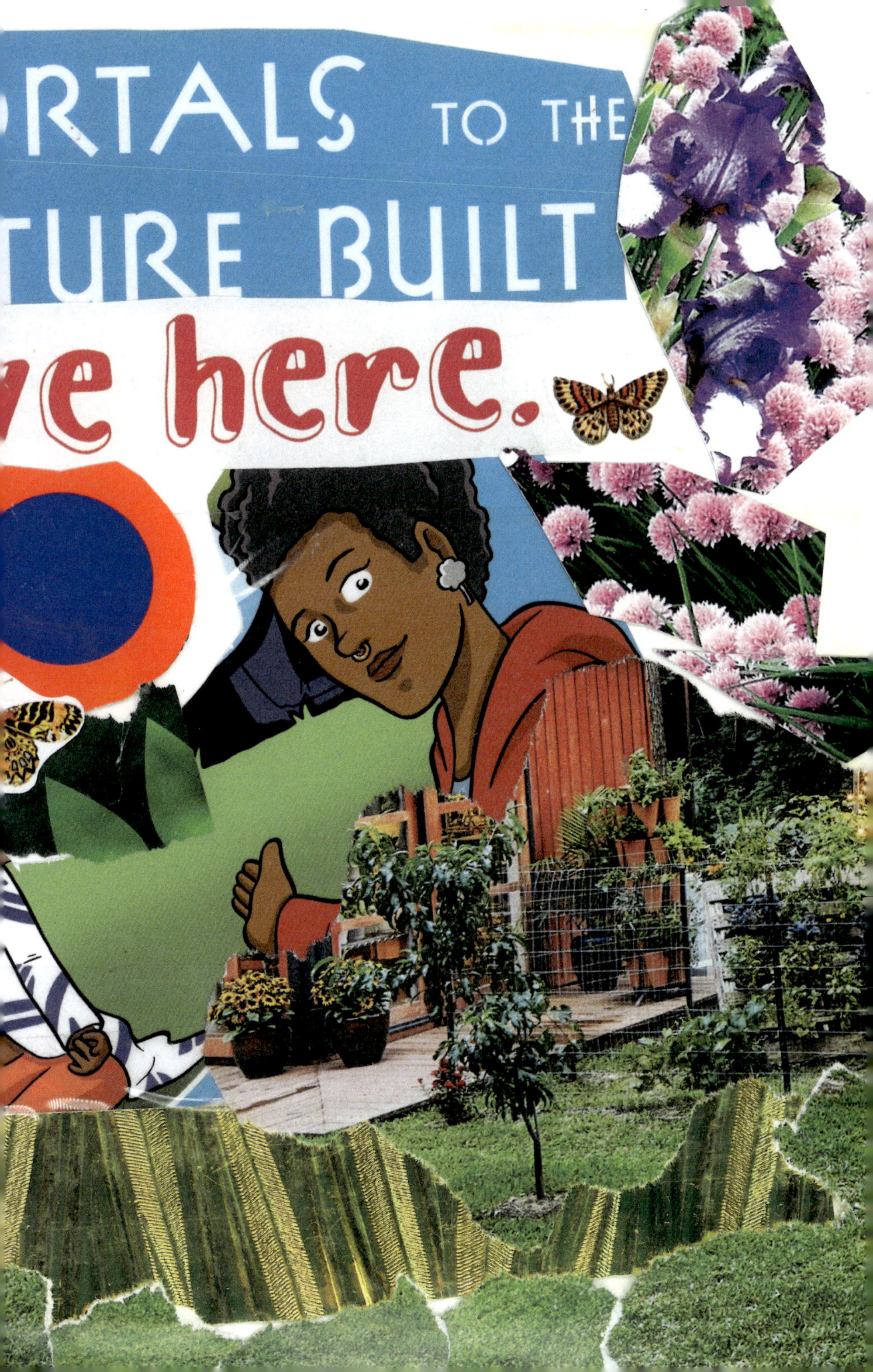
RTALS TO THE
TURE BUILT
ve here.

The Sacred Space of Nature and the Built Environment

Dail Chambers

How does land access connect us to our cultural heritage, family stories, and intergenerational economic growth?

I keep my relative and social narrative alive through daily interactions with the natural world. Weeding, planting trees, and observing and recording nature keeps my mind fresh with childhood memories, new information, and shared understandings. I connect the stories of loved ones to what foods I grow and eat, what flowers I cultivate, and what social art experiences I participate in. I archive material art objects, mixed with relics of sentiment and seed. Through land access, I have been privileged to actualize my dreams for humanity, create through community development, and make intergenerational shifts in my access to food production systems.

There are sentimental moments, when I am able to sit in a park-like environment that is intimate. Many days, my outdoor studio practice looks like observing flora and fauna in a field. I never knew this is what success, completion, or wholeness would look like for me until I experienced it one fall evening. Seeing myself in stillness and feeling good about it resourced the direction of my art. Land access has been the biggest gift to my own humanity, mental health, and nutrition.

When I began to identify as an artist, I prematurely associated the work with galleries, museums, and educational institutions. With the limited understanding of how land stewardship, access, and art broadens the potential of a creative person, I pursued each passion separately.

However, creating, responding to nature, and maintaining a natural environment has changed my perspective, values, social norms, and art practice. Through a new lens, engagement has expanded, and I am learning in public with the living environment around me.

Through my organizational stewardship with Yeyo Arts Collective, Civic Arts Development Corporation, and Coahoma Orchards Community Research Institute, I surveyed my neighbors and other residents through a cultural inquiry during the pandemic. The information I gathered informed what food crops and herbs I would grow on my sites, as I leaned into the hyperlocal expertise of the people who lived in the area before I entered. We started a mindfulness group and a nutritional awareness group, and I expanded my homestead to a multi-site food forest and educational farm project that is accessible to my neighbors and me.

Our community has long been highlighted for historical racism, segregation, food disparity, and violent erasure tactics. We recently withstood a devastating tornado. Through all these complex and rich experiences, I learned to trust the people who have shown up with shared interest and passion for creativity and nature. I also learned to trust the interactions of the people around me, developing my own truth of strength, resilience, and innovation.

During my time working with the *North St. Louis Creative Field Guide* working group, I've had the opportunity to offer some of these sentimental moments to my neighbors and community. As a group, we developed relationships that expand our own ecosystem of care, professionalism, and artmaking.

Our connection includes a mindfulness group, an agricultural study group, establishing community agreements with institutions in both the agricultural industry and through

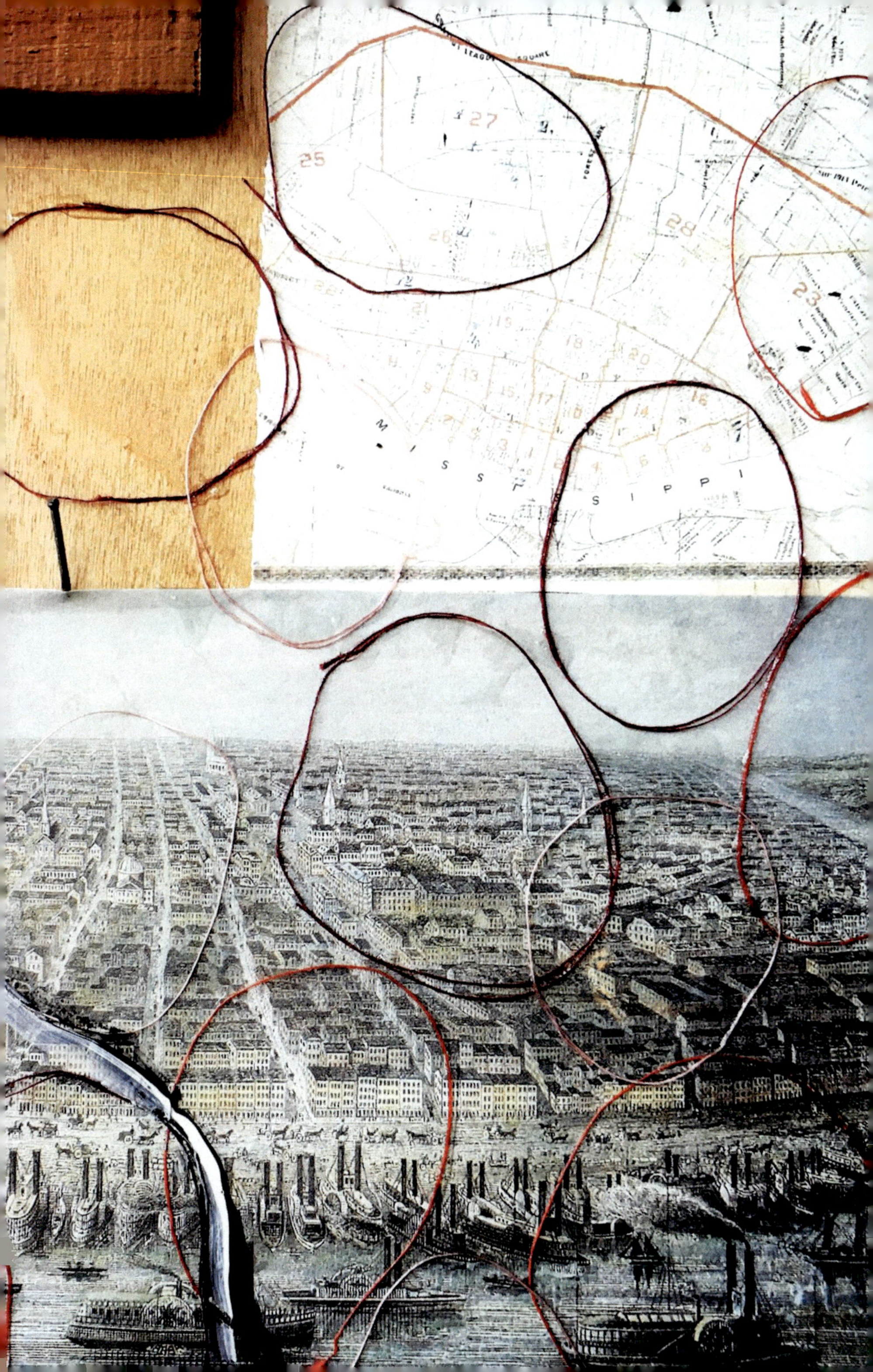

the *Field Guide*, and a multitude of workshops and public programs. We also honor a commitment to "water keeping," the advocacy, intentionality, and stewardship of our natural water sources. Reintegrating my practice to a communal experience has reinforced my own accountability agreements to the Earth.

I give appreciation to my fellow creative collaborators on this publication: AleXeana harlem, Alexis Creamer, Frankie Williams, Gabi Cole, Juan William Chávez, Kevin McCoy, Michelle Dezember, Rev. LaQuindlyn Shanae, Ronda Smith Branch, and Tosha Phonix.

We never know what experiences will impact us or change the course of our lives. As we gain more experiences with nature, whatever level we are at, new opportunities for growth and potential develop around us in the same way as the flowers bloom and trees fruit. That same sentiment can be applied to our work in built environment systems. When we align our lives to the natural process of nature, everything we work on, with and through the built environment, is small in comparison.

This work is dedicated to Ethel Mae Enoch Moore.

Seeds Collected During the Field Guide Project

Basil*
Bergamot/Bee balm
Black-eyed pea*
Carolina rose (from Northside Workshop)
Chia*
Coleus*
Coreopsis
Dill*
Echinacea
Elderberry
Jerusalem artichoke
Marigold*
Mountain mint (from Saundi McClain-Kloeckener)
Red cranberry bean
Snapdragon*
St. John's wort*
Sunflower
Zinnia

* Non-native

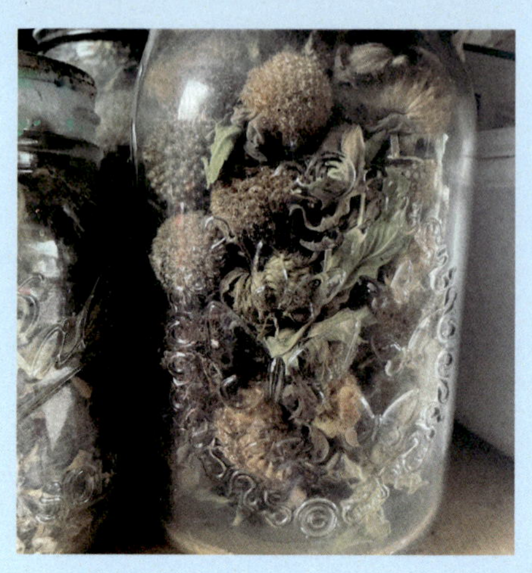

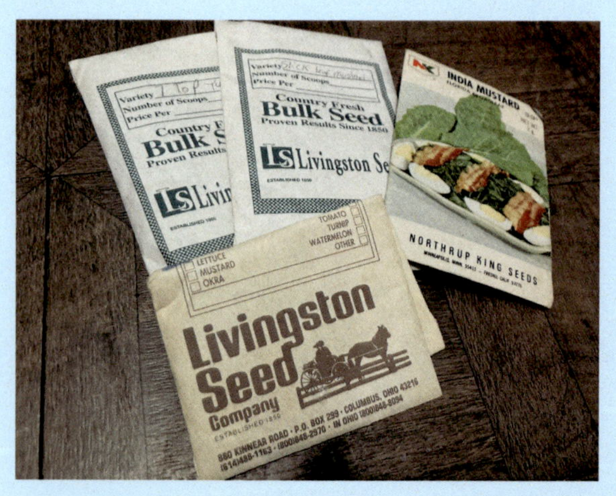
Variety
Number of Scoops
Price Per
Country Fresh
Bulk Seed
Proven Results Since 1850
LS Livingston Se
ESTABLISHED 1850
INDIA MUSTARD
NORTHRUP KING SEEDS
TOMATO
TURNIP
WATERMELON
OTHER
LETTUCE
MUSTARD
OKRA
Livingston
Seed
Company
ESTABLISHED 1850
880 KINNEAR ROAD · P.O. BOX 299 · COLUMBUS, OHIO 43216
(614)488-1163 · (800)848-2970 · IN OHIO (800)848-8094

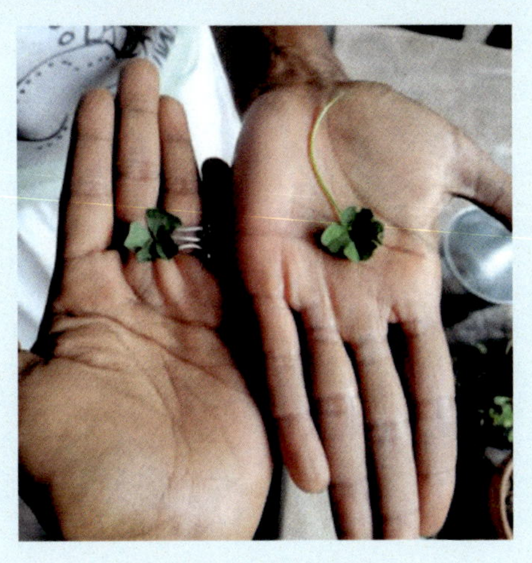

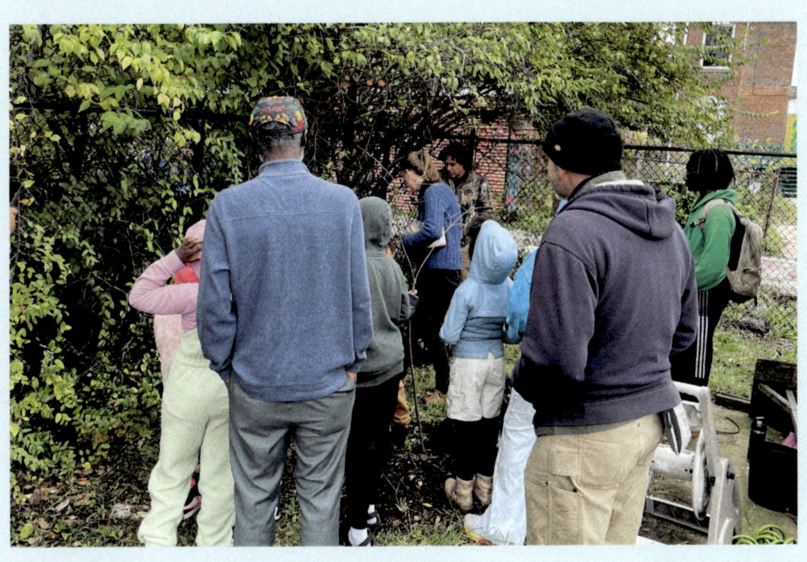

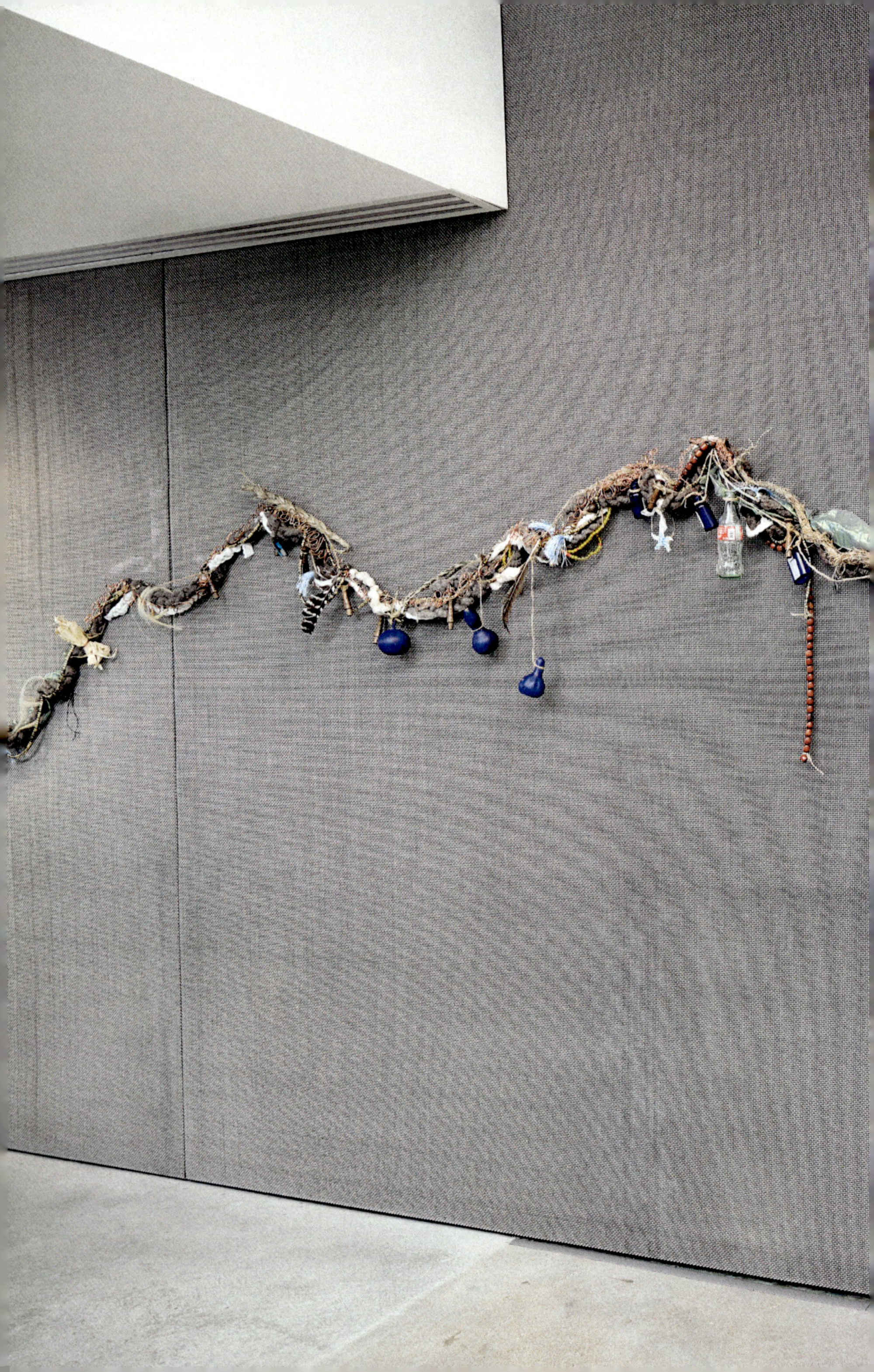

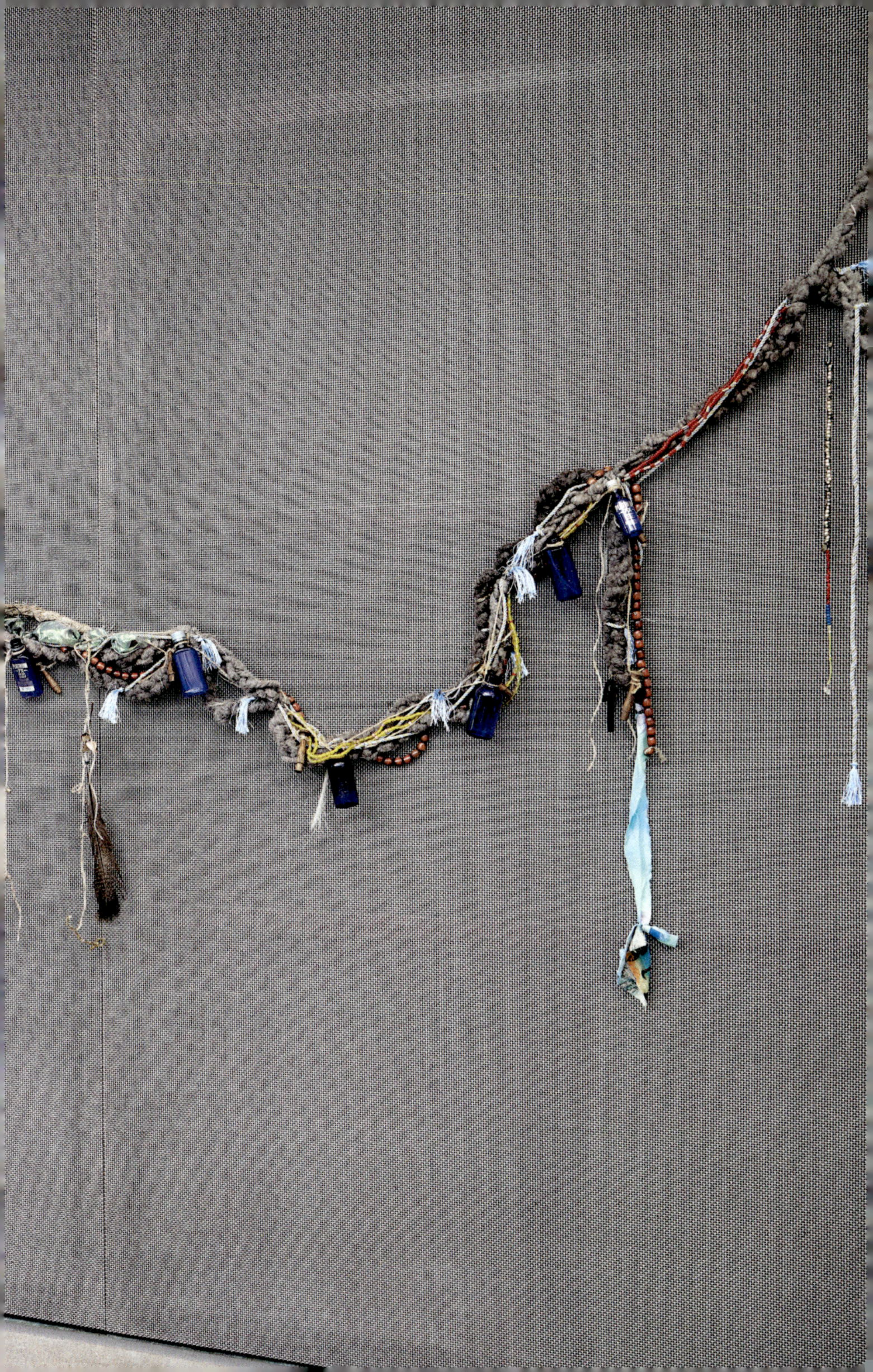

NOT A
NATIVE:
SNAPDRAGON
RED VELVET COLOR

ZINNIA
SEASONAL NATIVE
11/24

BERGAMOT
(BEE BALM)
NATIVE

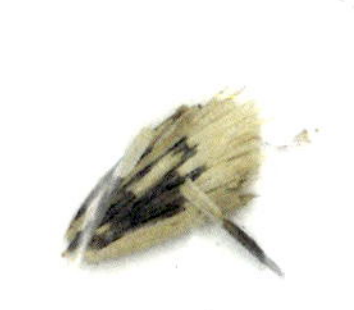

MARIGOLD
NOT QUITE NATIVE
* MIGRATION STORY

YELLOW NATIVE FLOWER
GIFTED FROM DRUSILLA
IN MISSISSIPPI—MAILED
11/24
(IN AND OUT OF
NAPKIN IT
WAS
WRAPPED
IN.)

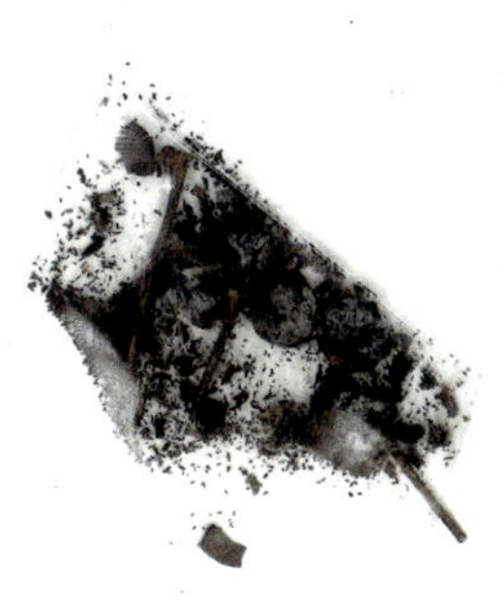

ELDERBERRY

FROM NORTHSIDE WORKSHOP 12/18

WHAT PLANT IS THIS FROM FOUNTAIN PARK 2024?

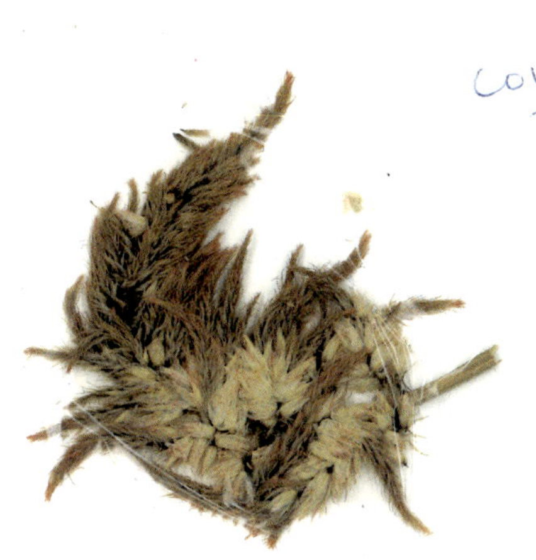

COLEUS?
TOSHAS FARM/
ETHELS
HOUSE

MOUNTAIN MINT
FROM SAUNDI

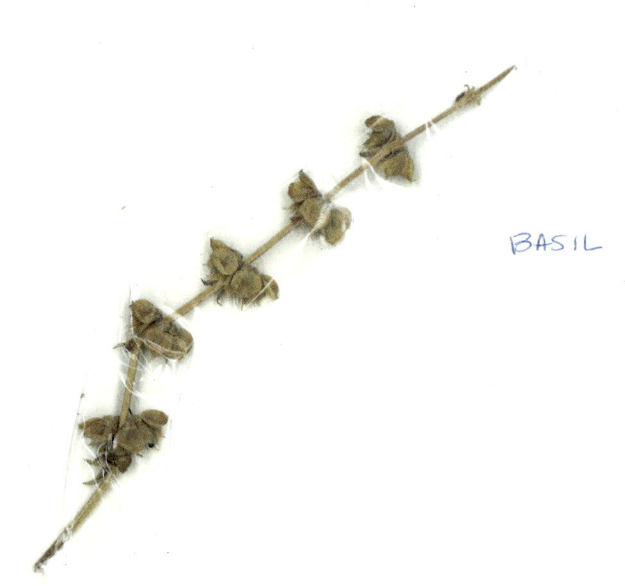
BASIL

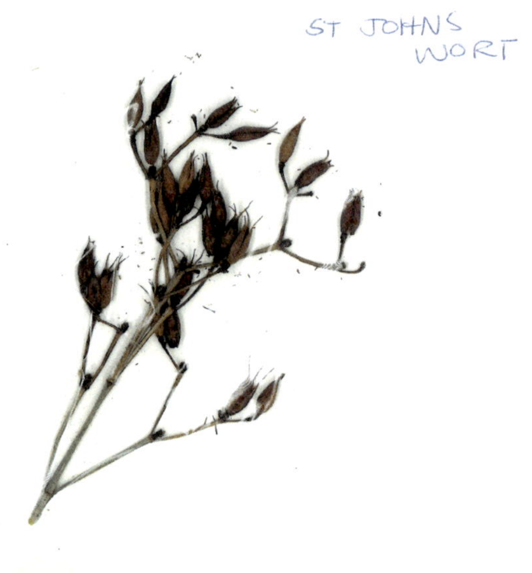
ST JOHNS WORT

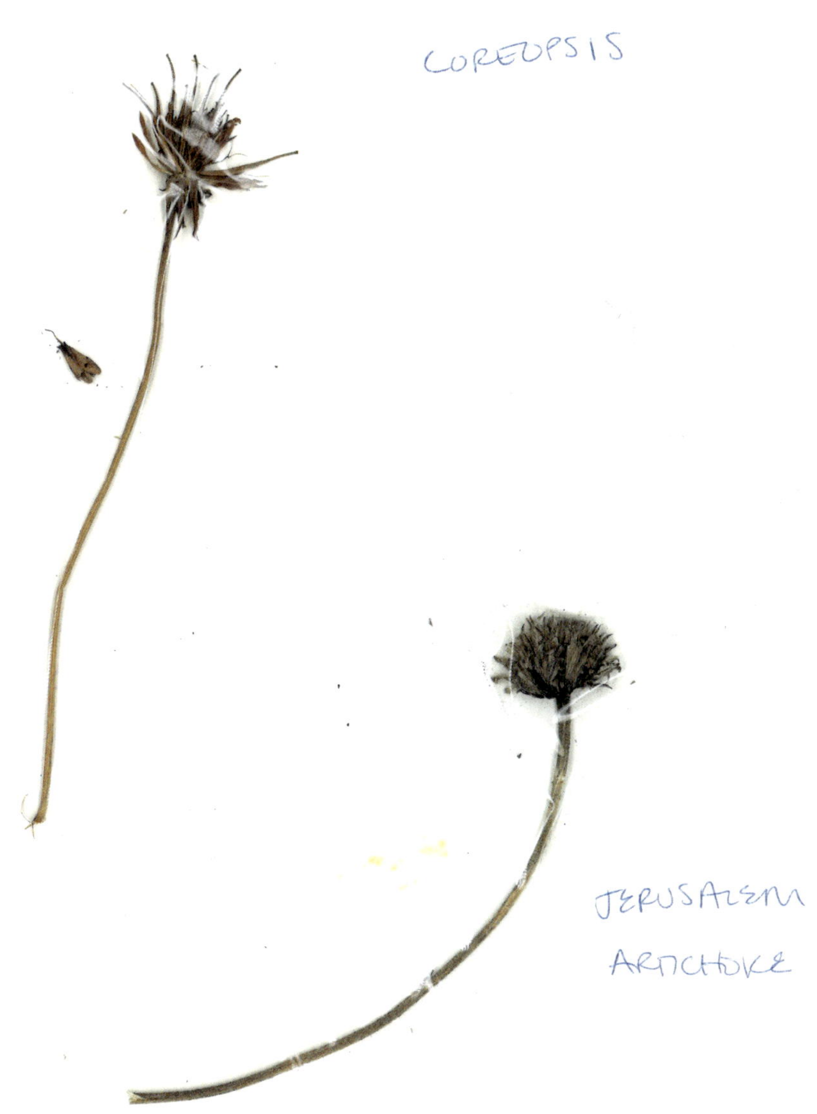
COREOPSIS
JERUSALEM
ARTICHOKE

COTTON FROM
LYONS MISSISSIPPI

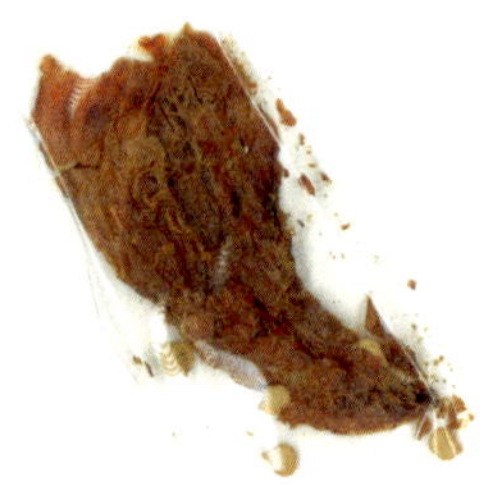

Red Pepper
from Backyard
garden.

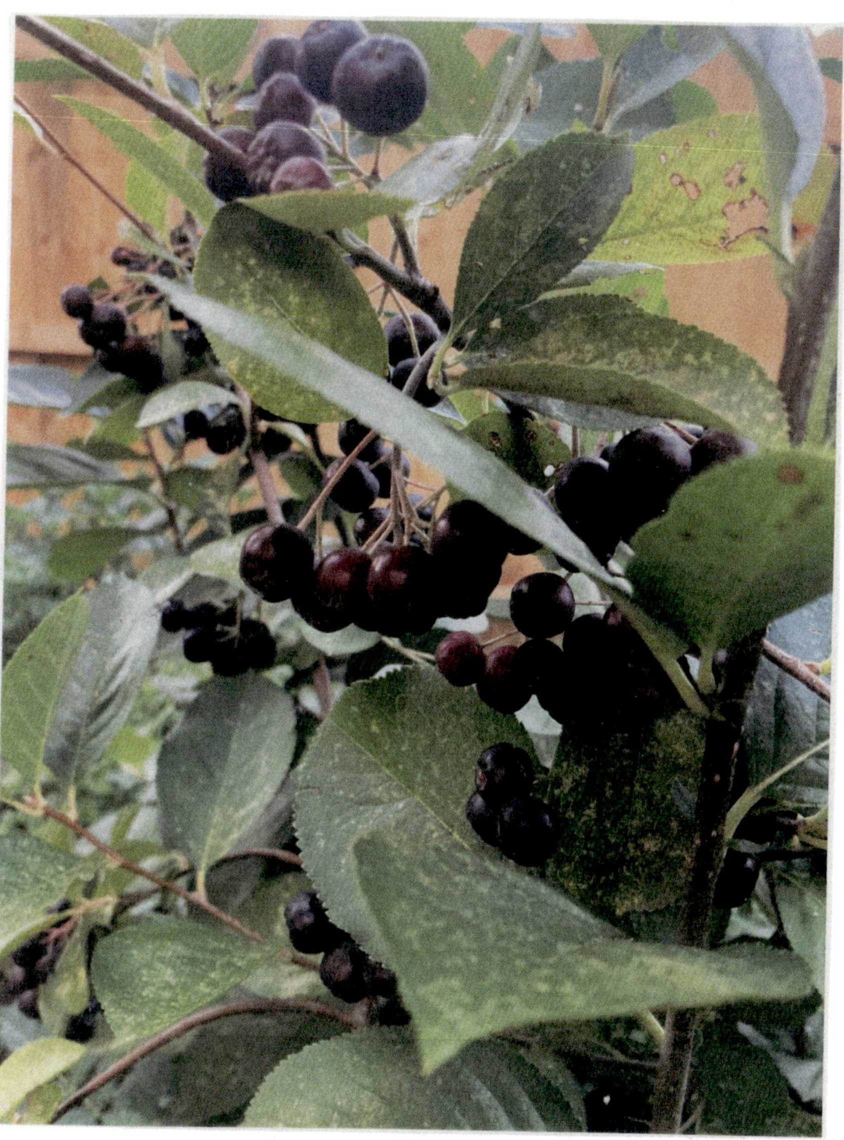

CHOKEBERRY AT MINDFULNESS SITE

The Garden as an Art Studio

Juan William Chávez

Since 2012, my social practice art has focused on environmental and food rights in North St. Louis. As the founder and director of the Northside Workshop, a nonprofit organization focused on art and ecology, I collaborate with Master Gardener Kiersten Torrez. Together we have implemented experiential workshops, cultivated a chemical-free teaching garden, and established a native bee sanctuary within the Old North St. Louis neighborhood, encouraging community engagement with nature.

Decolonize the Hive and Garden

Our teaching garden and bee sanctuary emphasize Indigenous growing practices to address the colonial roots often associated with gardening. We strive to move away from designs that were historically rooted in the labor of servants and enslaved individuals. Our efforts focus on creating a chemical-free environment that mimics and embraces the native ecosystem.
This commitment has cultivated a habitat for nearly 200 species of native bees found in St. Louis and over 150 native plant species located on-site. We offer workshops that focus on self-expression, environmental stewardship, and community building, covering topics such as creating native bee habitats, growing edible landscapes, and the importance of native plants. Participants engage in hands-on activities, crafting gardening aprons from upcycled T-shirts, planting native species in take-home grow bags, and walking tours that stimulate the senses through sight, sound, touch, smell, and taste.

Pollinator Press: Zines

Our workshops are compiled into zines and artists' posters produced by our in-house risograph printer, Northside Workshop's Pollinator Press. These zines facilitate knowledge sharing and provide prompts with calls to action, encouraging individuals to creatively explore their own green spaces.

North St. Louis Creative Field Guide

My passion for almanacs inspired the idea of creating an almanac-like book that integrates art and gardening, specifically for North St. Louis. Michelle Dezember and I worked on a past initiative, Growing Safe Spaces, which included a tour of North St. Louis City gardens and a workshop focused on native bees and native plants. Michelle's strengths in collaboration and problem-solving made our partnership immensely fruitful, and we discovered a shared interest in almanacs during this time.

Our mutual interest naturally led to exploring the art almanac concept, building on the groundwork we established during Growing Safe Spaces. As we pursued this vision, it became clear that the project would be an excellent fit for a National Endowment for the Arts (NEA) Our Town grant.

Once the project was awarded this grant, we invited artist Dail Chambers to serve as one of the lead artists, advancing the project to the next level. I have long admired Dail's work and vision, and collaborating with her felt like a perfect opportunity to celebrate her practice. We share similar aesthetics and values in our community-building efforts, making this collaboration particularly meaningful.

As one of the lead artists, I embodied multiple roles within this project. I worked alongside Michelle to develop the project proposal and collaborated with Dail to create categories for the *Field Guide* that related to her artistic practice. I lead workshops focused on creativity, native bees, and native plants while listening to and mentoring members of our cohort. Additionally, I contributed to the *Field Guide* by crafting a zine that honors the life and work of Charles Henry Turner, a pioneering American entomologist known for his insightful studies on insect behavior, who taught at Sumner High School in The Ville neighborhood of North St. Louis.

Northside Workshop's Garden Tour: A Memorable Moment
The garden, regardless of season, is a magical space filled with life and interaction. One particularly fond memory from winter was hosting the *Field Guide* cohort at Northside Workshop. Despite the garden being in hibernation, magic unfolded when a bald eagle soared above us—a rare sight in my fourteen years there. Its majestic presence ignited joy and excitement among the group, including some "expressive" cheers. This moment perfectly encapsulated the connection and happiness we all shared as we explored the intersection of art and gardening together.

I have a deep respect and appreciation for everyone who has worked on this project. Thank you to Dail Chambers, Michelle Dezember, Alexis Creamer, and the phenomenal cohort. I learned a great deal from each of you. And my gratitude to the staff at CAM for their support in making the *North St. Louis Creative Field Guide* possible.

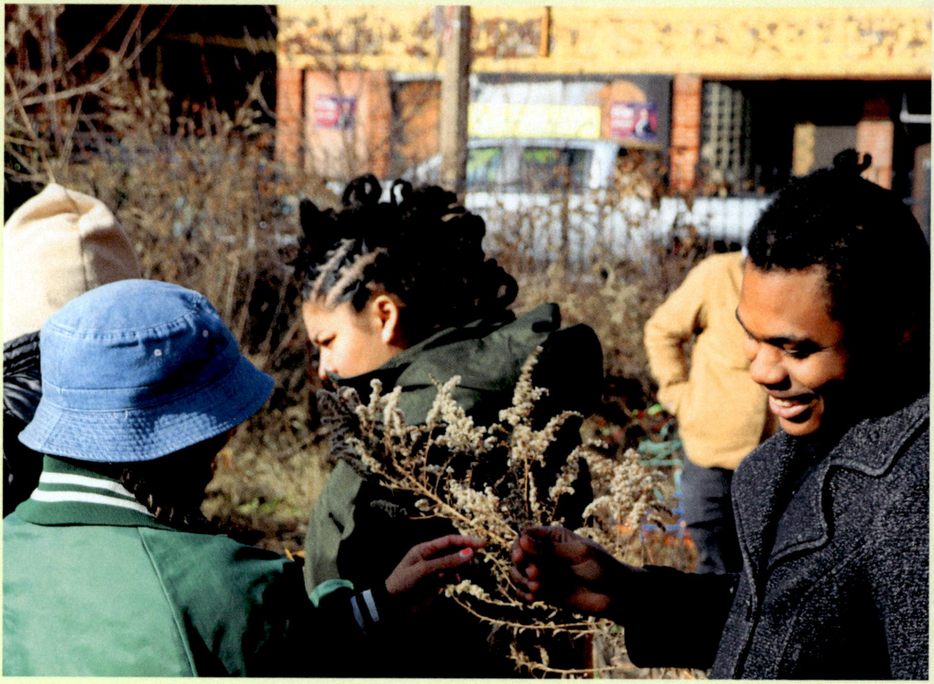

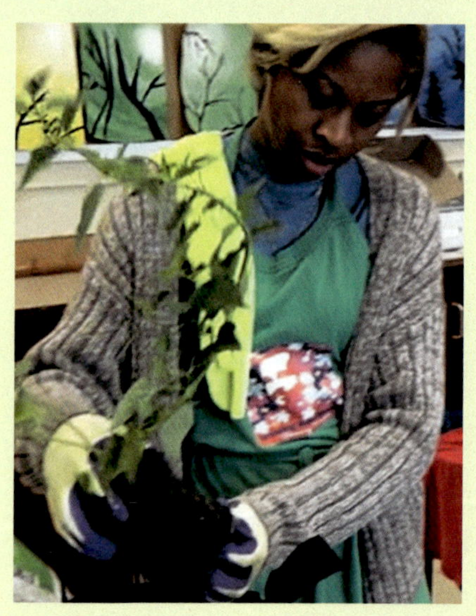

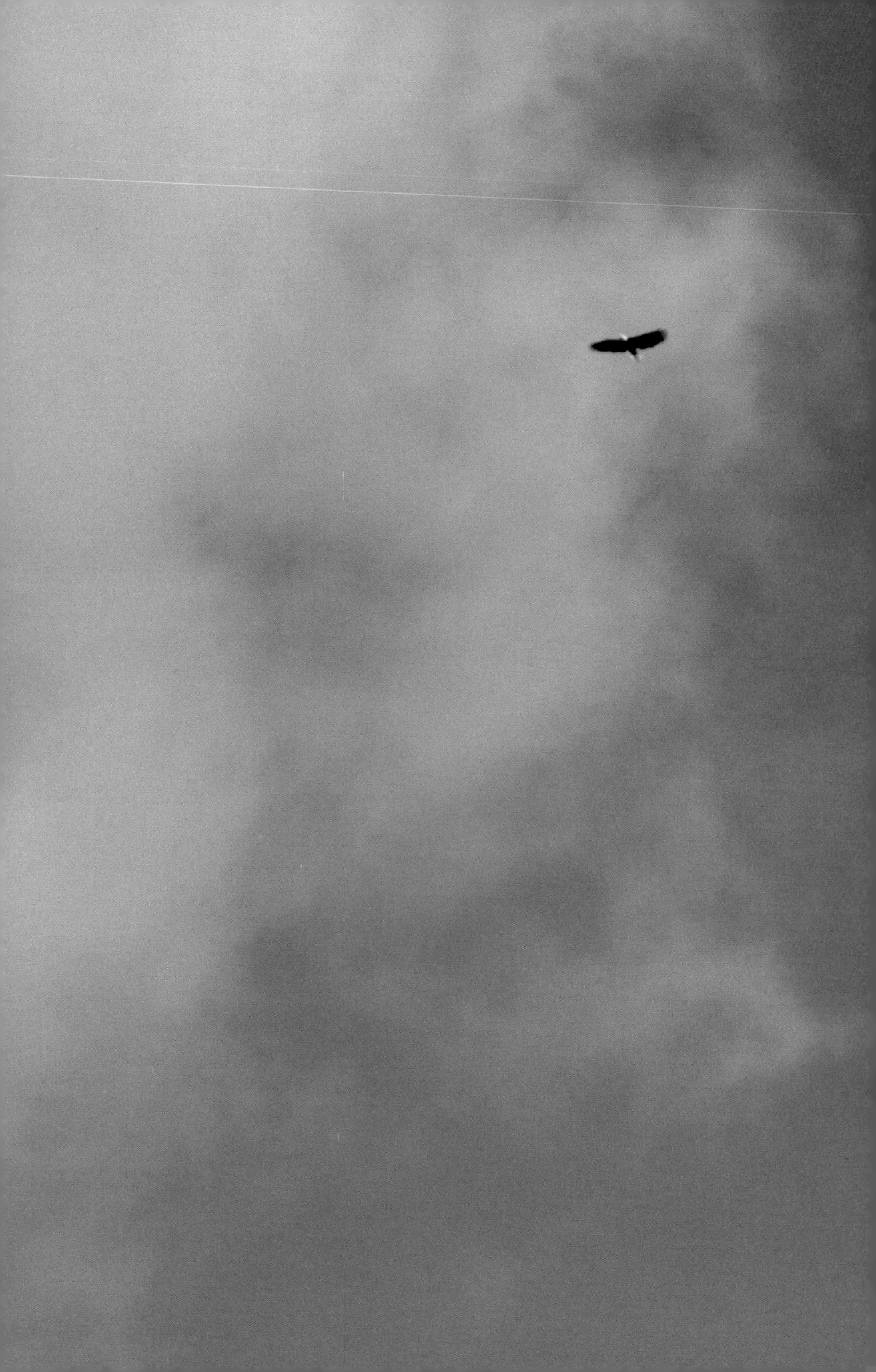

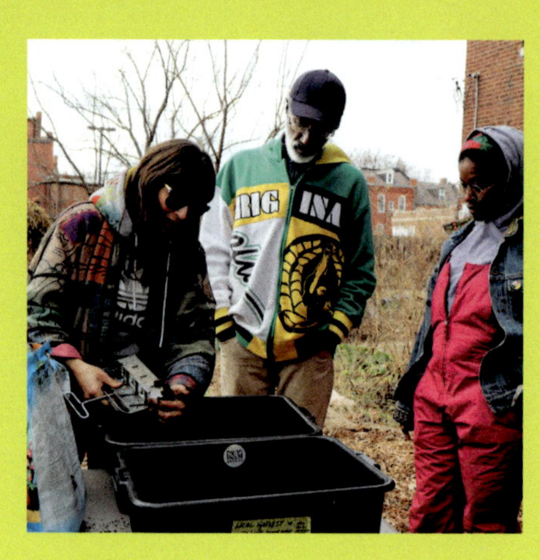

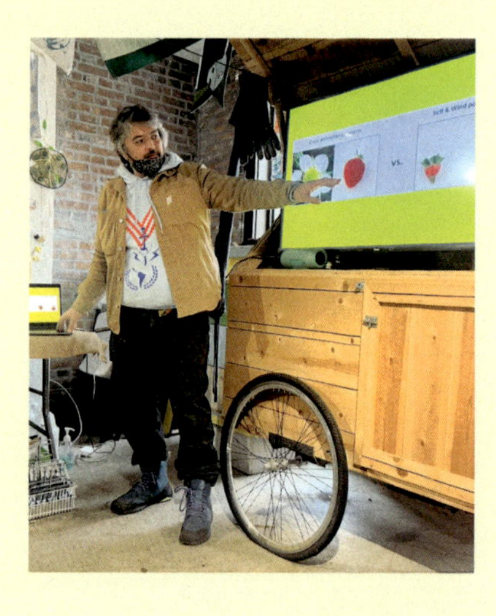

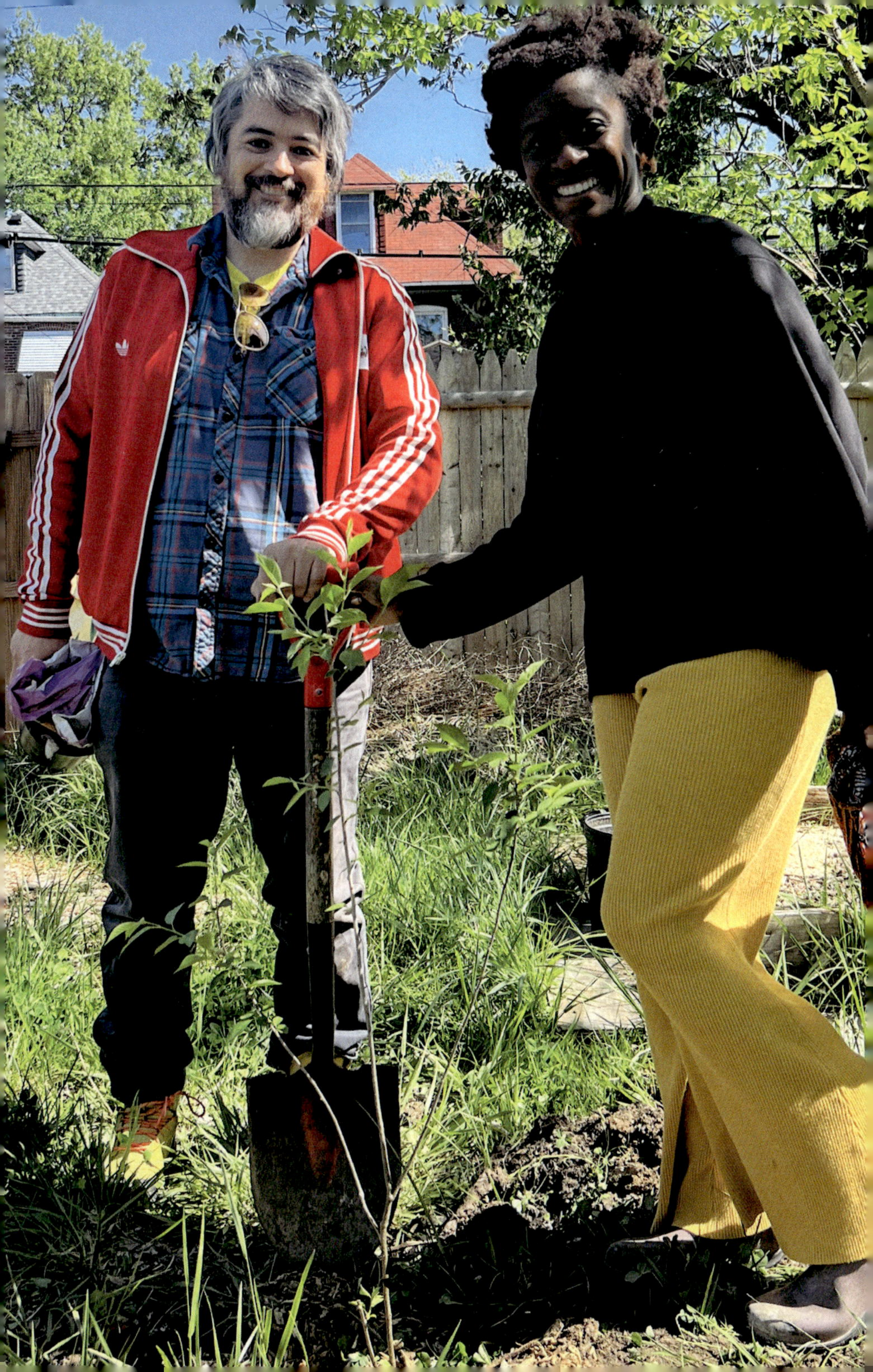

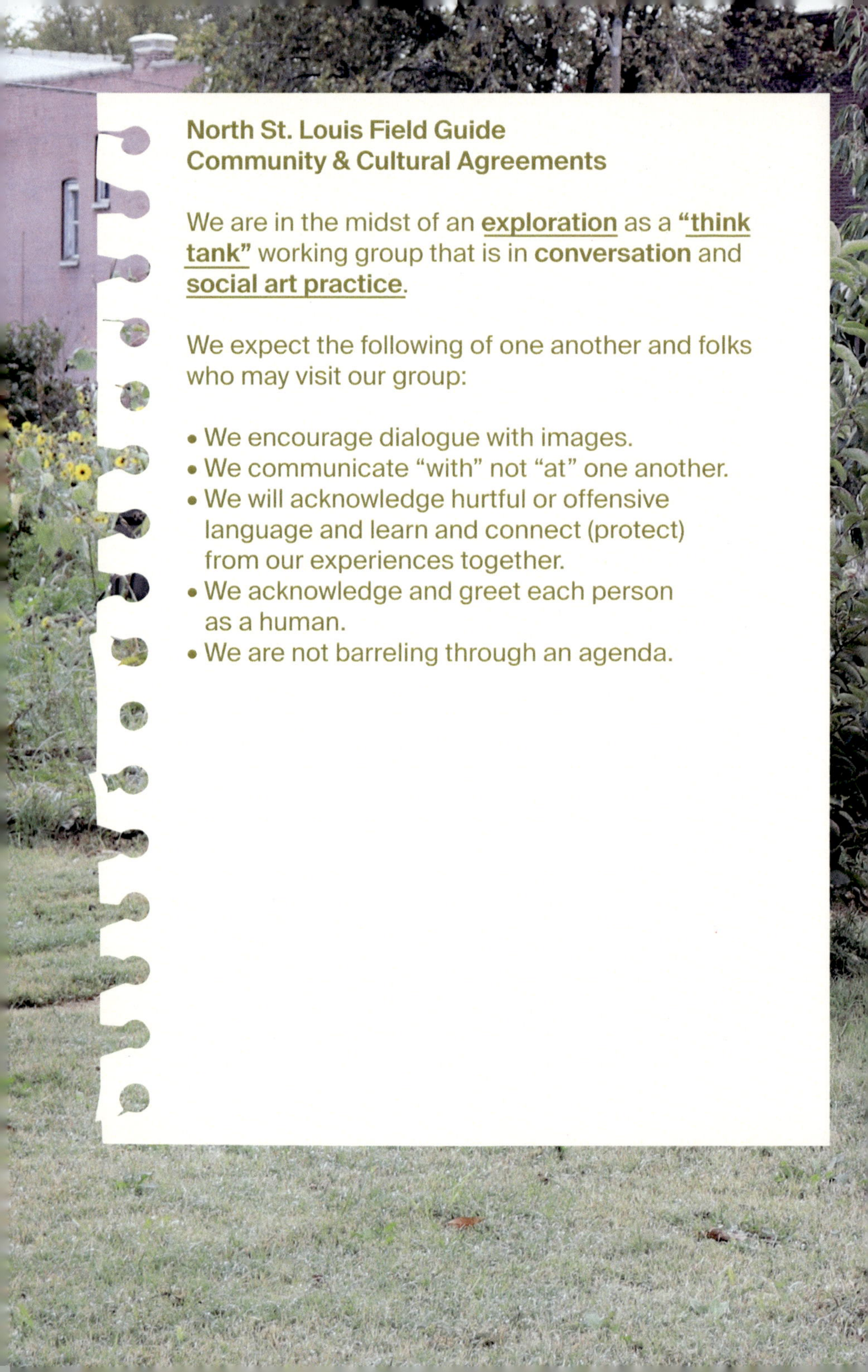

North St. Louis Field Guide
Community & Cultural Agreements

We are in the midst of an **exploration** as a **"think tank"** working group that is in **conversation** and **social art practice**.

We expect the following of one another and folks who may visit our group:

- We encourage dialogue with images.
- We communicate "with" not "at" one another.
- We will acknowledge hurtful or offensive language and learn and connect (protect) from our experiences together.
- We acknowledge and greet each person as a human.
- We are not barreling through an agenda.

Other practices that help us show up as our best selves in shared spaces...

- Open mind
- Reflection on impact vs. intent
- Assertiveness
- Hospitable attitude
- Asking over assuming
- Accountability (take it and require it)
- Tell the truth
- Be respectful and self aware
- Choose the lens of love
- Acceptance
- We should make direct eye contact and speak to one another
- Hold a space of spiritual/conscious/creative safety by using tolerance and acceptance when critiquing, dialogue, and group discussion
- Space to trust
- Set group intentions
- Be in reflection (group and as individual)
- Trust lived experience
- Awareness and knowledge of who is in space in person and virtual (at the point of interest)

* These agreements were cocreated over several sessions by the working group, and serve as an invitation to how we encourage the continuation of this work.

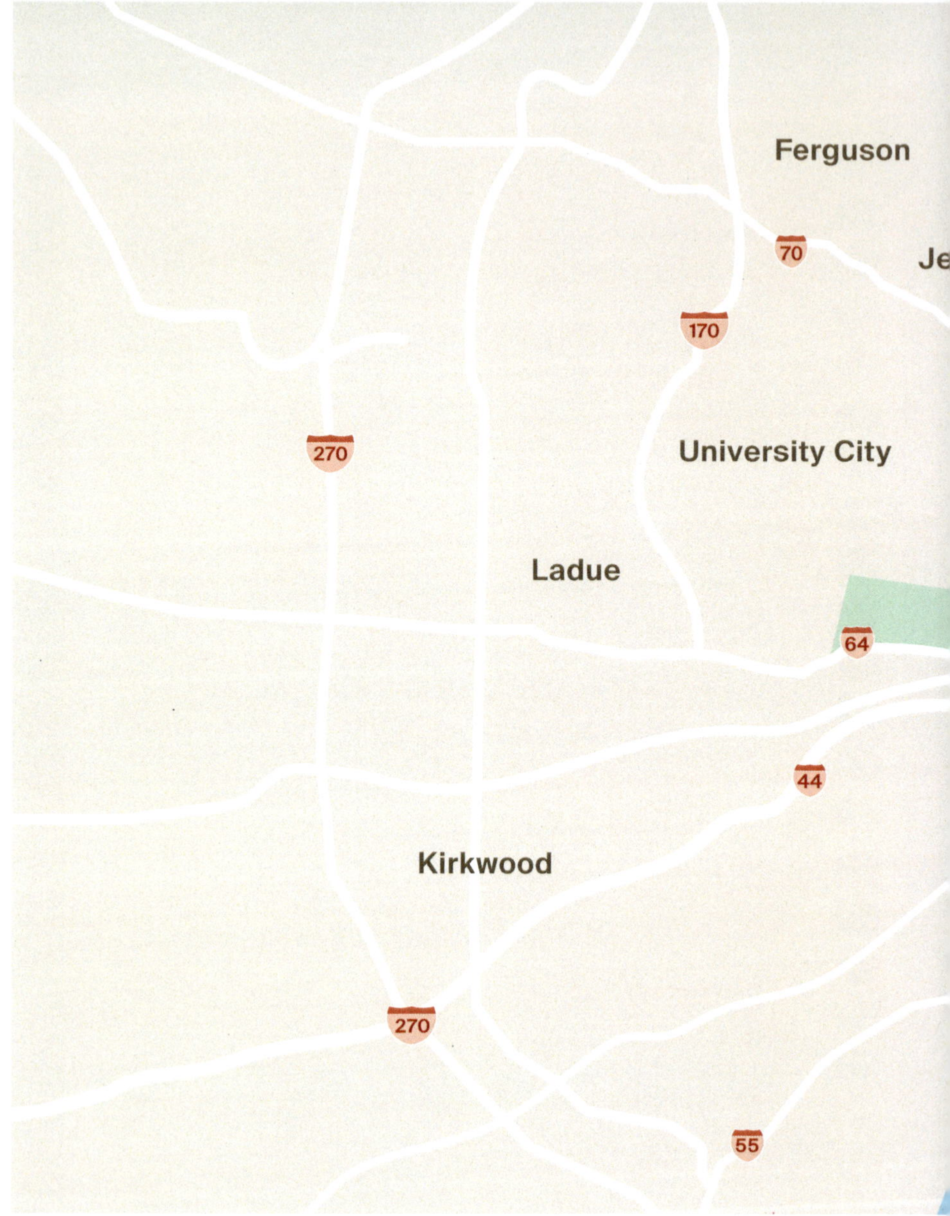

SITES REFERENCED IN NORTH ST. LOUIS CREATIVE FIELD GUIDE

- Fit & Food Connection [4846 St. Louis Ave]
- Sumner High School [4248 Cottage Ave]
- A.C.R.E.S. [5007 Genevieve Ave]
- Contemporary Art Museum St. Louis [3750 Washington Blvd]
- Northside Workshop [1306 St. Louis Ave]
- Coahoma Orchards Community Research Institute [3901 Labadie Ave]

Mississippi River

Granite City

70

70

St. Louis

Mississippi River

SSOURI

ILLINOIS

Dupo

- Cahokia Mounds State Historic Site
- Fairground Park
- O'Fallon Park

Charles Henry Turner: Garden as a Laboratory

Juan William Chávez

Charles Henry Turner (1867–1923) was a renowned zoologist and pioneering figure in studying insect behavior. His research, primarily conducted at O'Fallon Park in North St. Louis, resulted in the publication of forty-nine papers on various invertebrates, including notable works on ants and honeybees. His innovative findings revealed that insects are capable of performing complex behaviors and learning, such as recognizing visual patterns and navigating using landmarks. Turner's work, which was revolutionary for its time, advocated for a cognitive approach to understanding animal behavior. He emphasized the role of memory and learning in insects, challenging the notion that their actions were purely instinctual.

In 2024, Northside Workshop hosted an art and gardening workshop at Sumner High School titled "Growing Safe Spaces: Honoring Turner." This event celebrated the influential entomology work of Turner, who taught at Sumner from 1908 to 1922. The workshop highlighted how he ingeniously utilized the public green space of O'Fallon Park for groundbreaking research on insect behavior with a particular focus on bees. By bridging the realms of art, science, and education, the workshop honored Turner's enduring legacy and inspired future generations to build upon his groundbreaking insights.

Participants in the workshop engaged in a hands-on experience, viewing the garden as a laboratory. They crafted personalized gardening aprons, planted native species in take-home grow bags, and learned about plant anatomy and the vital role of pollinators. This collaborative effort between Northside Workshop and CAM aimed to link art with science and foster a deeper appreciation for both disciplines. An exciting addition to the workshop was the involvement of artist and designer LM Flowers, who worked with Sumner students to design a logo featured on the aprons that reflected their connection to Turner's legacy. The workshop also inspired the creation of a zine about Turner for the *North St. Louis Creative Field Guide*.

Scan to download the zine
Charles Henry Turner: Garden as a Laboratory (2025)

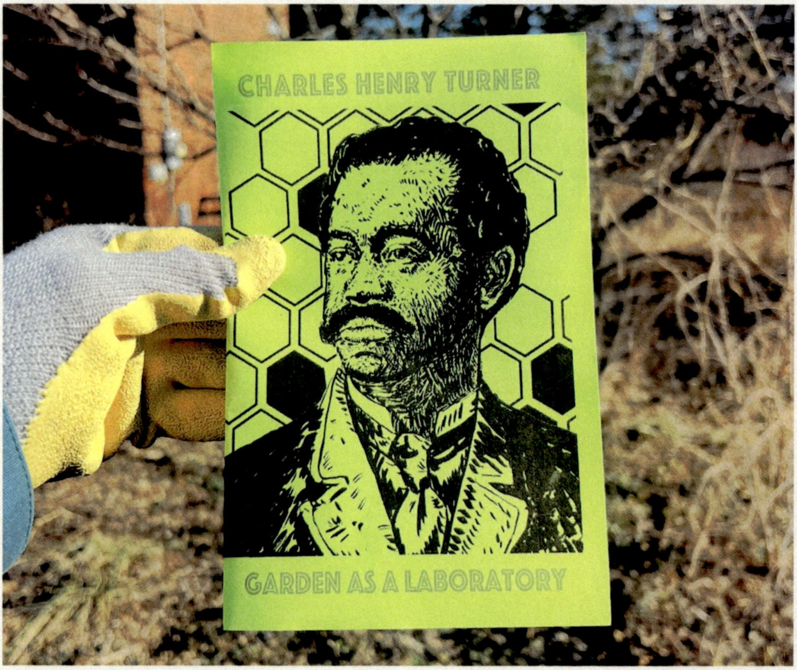

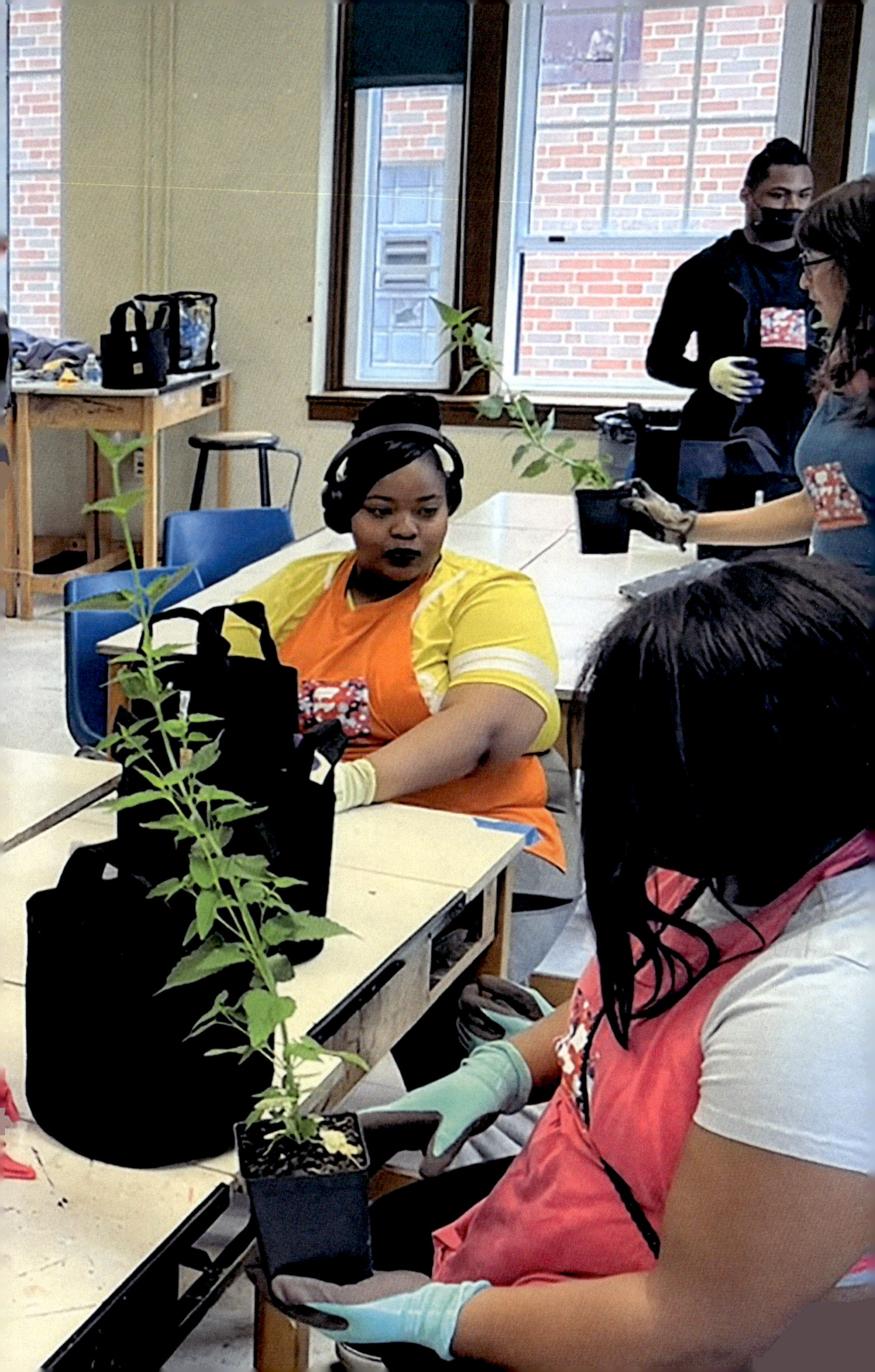

POLLINATION APRON

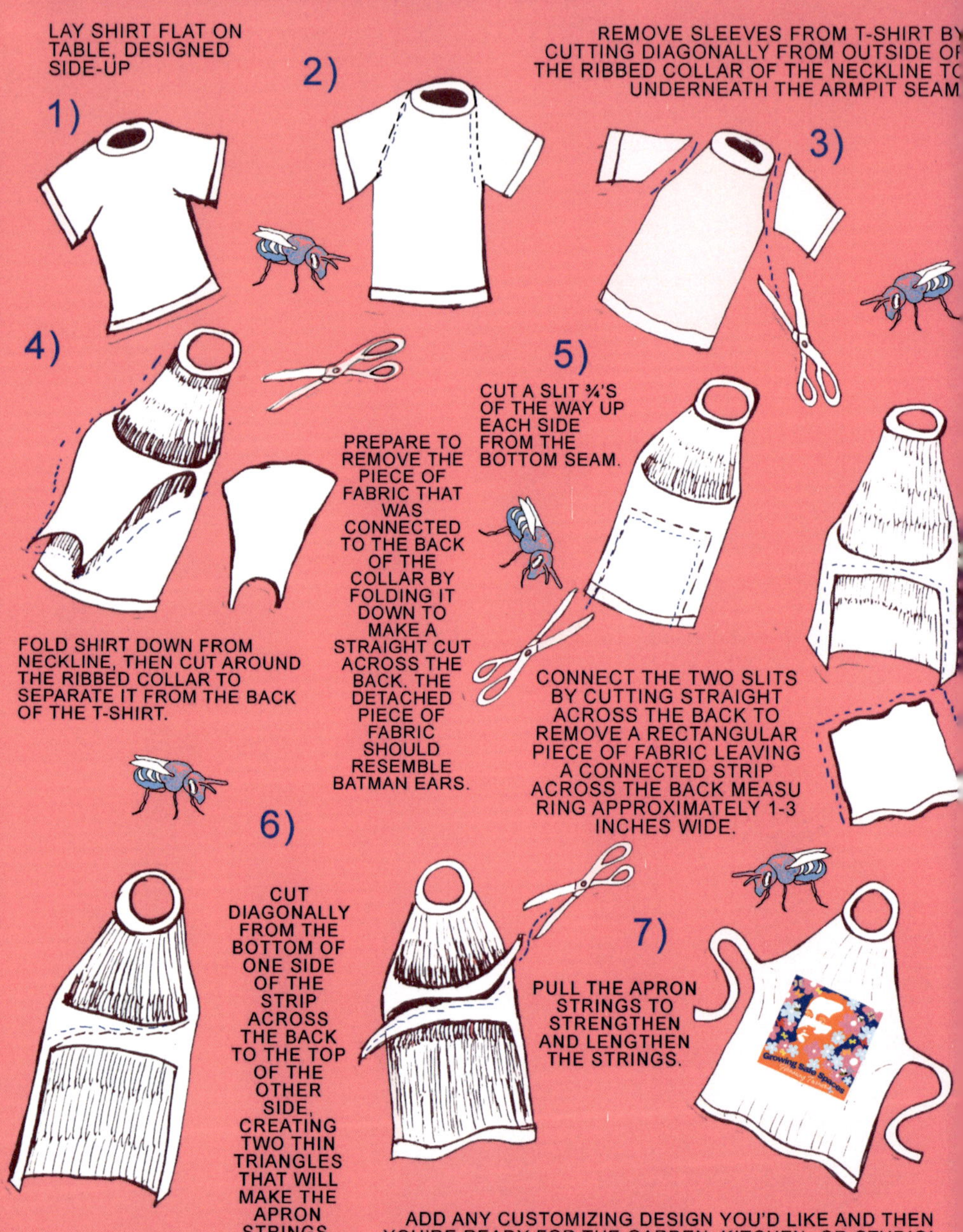

A CREATIVE REUSE FOR COOKING AND GARDENING

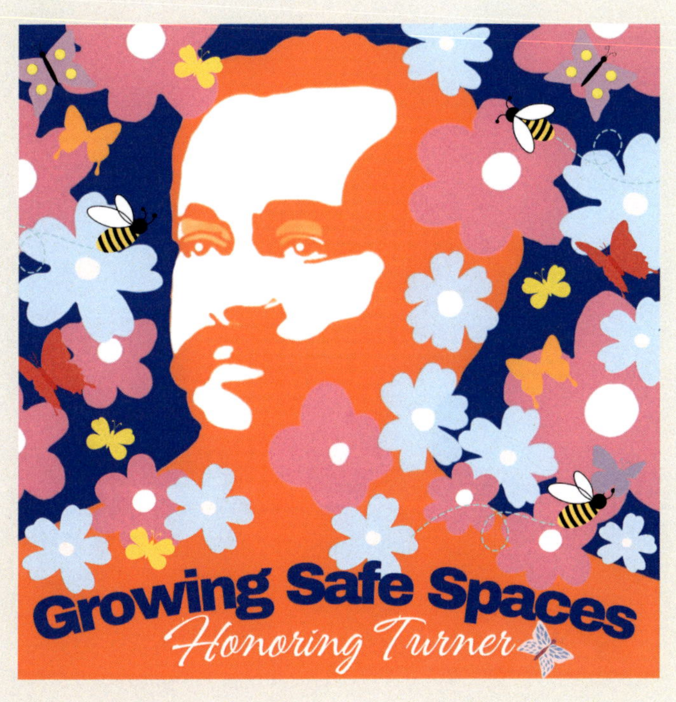
Growing Safe Spaces
Honoring Turner

Finding Our Way: Home in North St. Louis

AleXeana harlem

North St. Louis City stands as a beautiful paradox. For outsiders, it reads as a wasteland, crime-ridden, blighted by decades of intentional disinvestment. For those of us who call it home, we carry a different story: a narrative of a beautiful existence, care as resistance, and love for our neighborhood and community. My work *Our Ancestors' Compass Points North* (2025) exists as a thank you to my first St. Louis home, a recording of North St. Louis from those that love her, the time travel that occurs there, and a map to the way back home.

For these pieces, I went into my neighborhood to learn from fellow North St. Louis residents. Building on these interviews, I combined photography, cyanotype, weaving, digital design, textile creation, and sewing to create *Our Ancestors' Compass Points North*.

Our Ancestors' Compass Points North exists in four parts:

Part One is a stretched cotton map hung to canvas. The map showcases different neighborhoods in North St. Louis and the Guardian protectors that watch over the land. I have also included sigils, symbols and icons that serve as protection, watching over the neighborhood.

Parts Two through Four are time totems. These soft sculptures are composed of cotton that is printed on and embroidered with beads and found objects. The totems stand as identification markers and wayfinding tools to the portals of our neighborhood. These landmarks have refused to be bound by linear time and oppressive systems, standing as signifiers of the way home.

Past care and ancestor veneration has set the foundation for current wholeness and future prosperity. To care for the future, we look toward the past, collapsing boundaries of space and time to manifest a safe, prosperous reality in the now.

It is my hope that *Our Ancestors' Compass Points North* carries forward past:present:future care for you.

> My heart knows home,
> for I am made of home.
> Where else must I seek,
> when the home is in me?

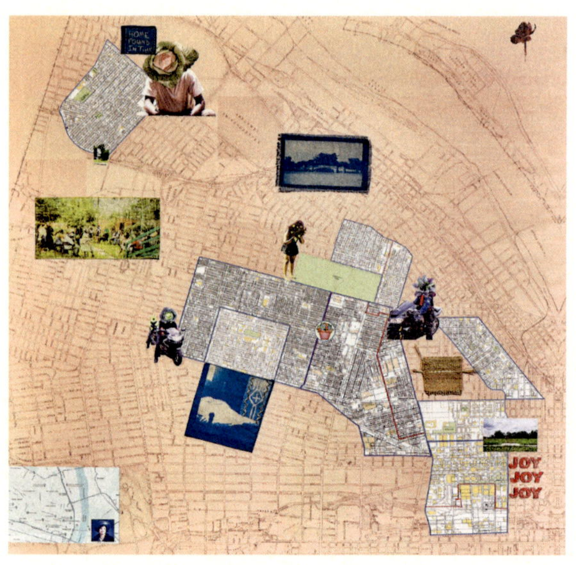

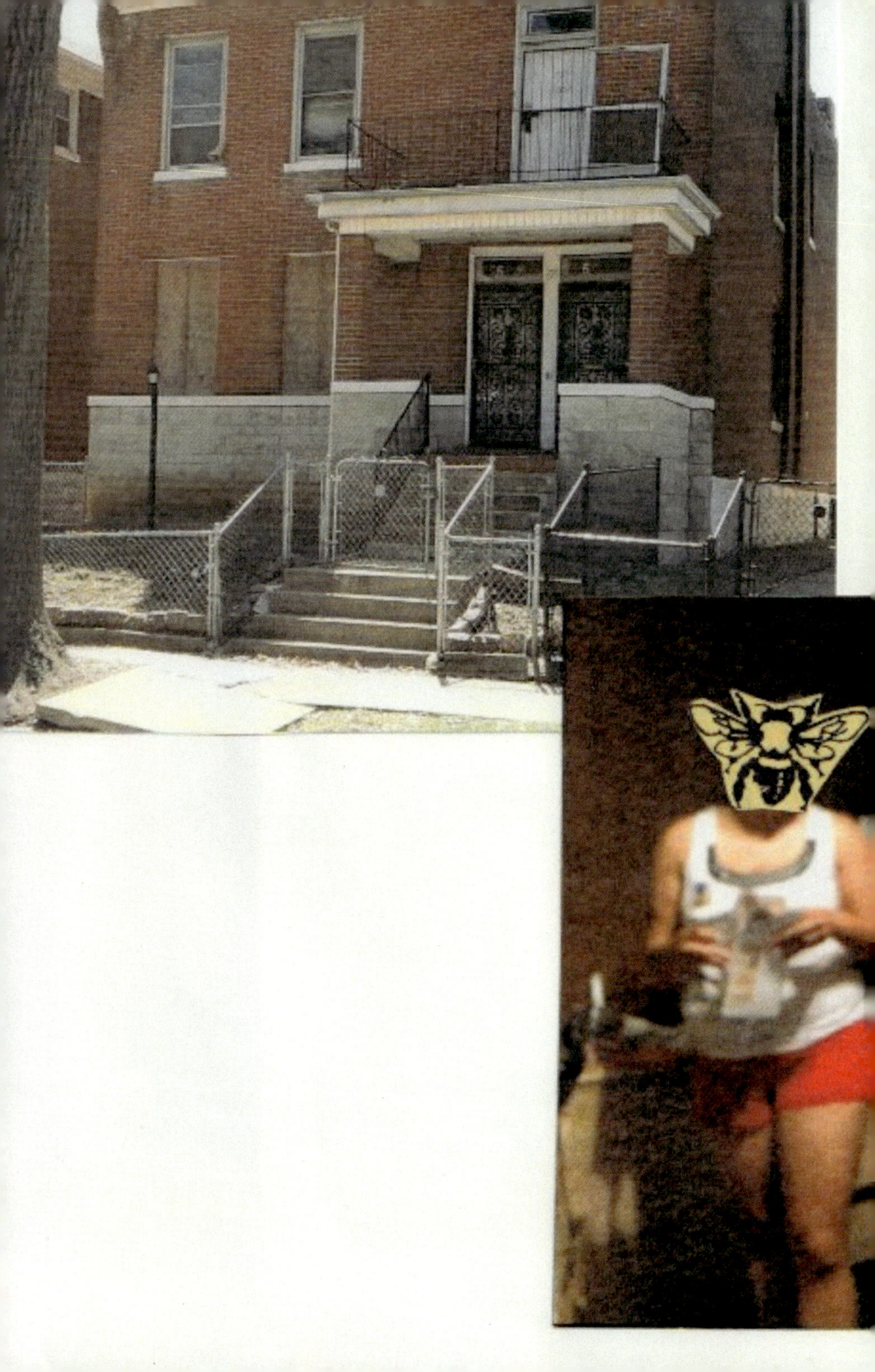

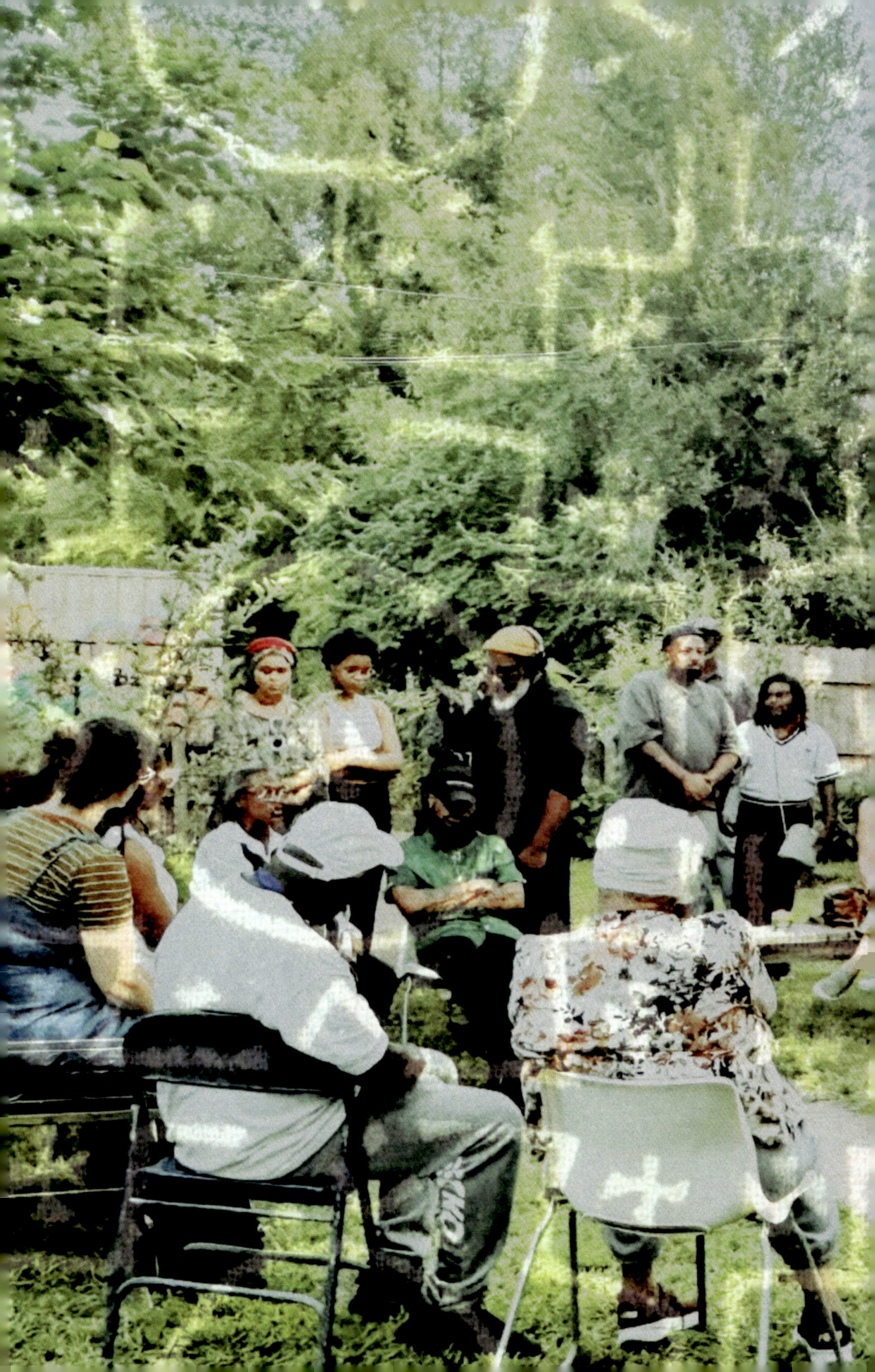

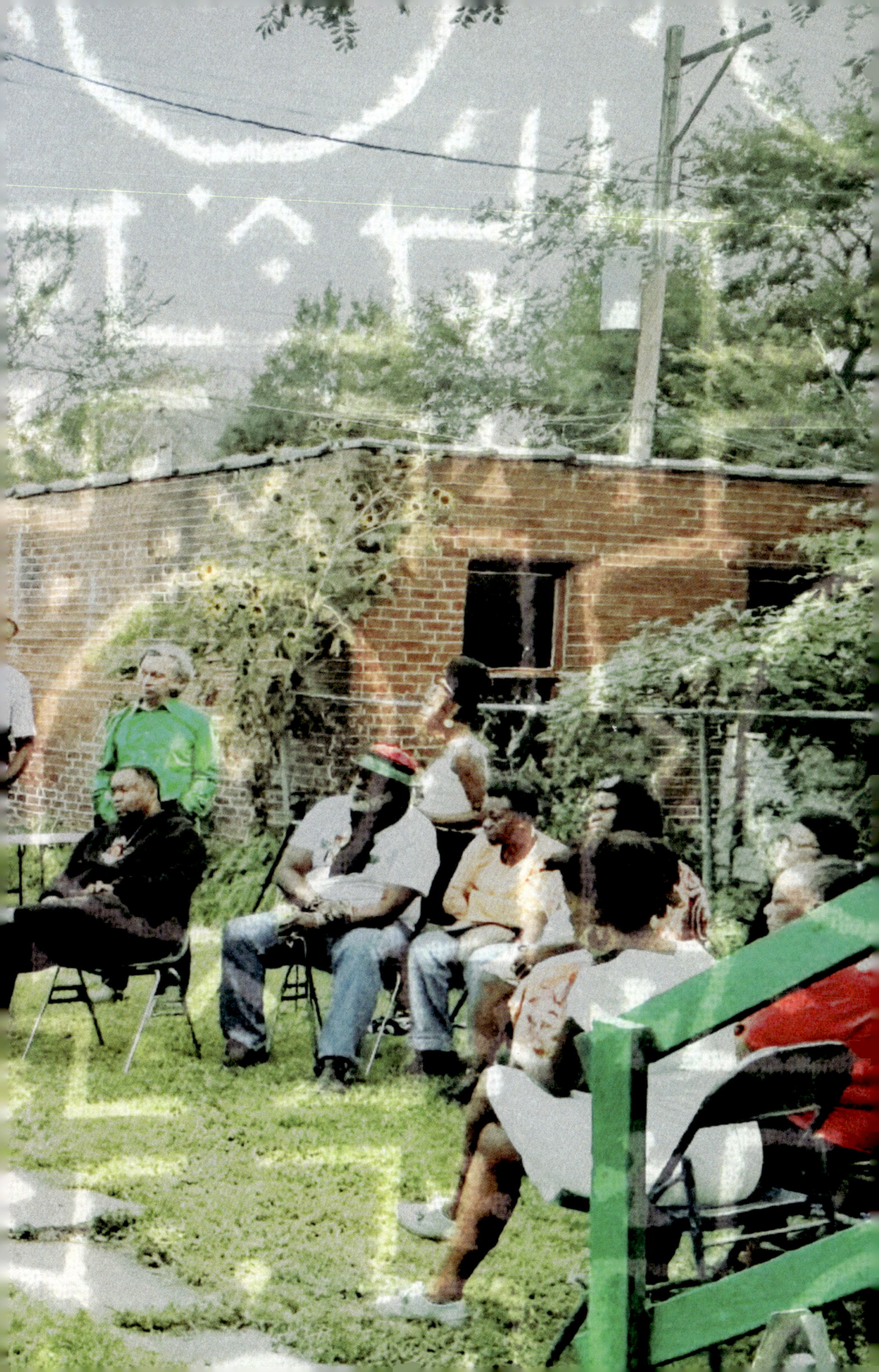

We're All Together

Frankie Williams

I've lived in The Ville neighborhood my whole life, and it's where my family has been even before I was born. I love how peaceful it is and how I can actually talk to my neighbors—some of them I've known for years. So, when the tornado on May 16, 2025, destroyed my family's house and forced us to move to temporary housing outside the city, I was worried we might leave forever. After we received support from friends, family, and colleagues, and moved into our new home back in The Ville, I wanted to make an artwork that not only represented how I got through this struggle, but also how we can all navigate hard times.

I created a mural called *We're All Together* (2025) that represents how my community helped me get through tough times after the tornado and how I am generally someone with complex emotions. At the center of the painting is a black rose, which represents me. Red roses can mean love, but I chose black because it matches the gloomy, dark feelings I have sometimes. I wear black clothes a lot and I'm sensitive to topics that can feel heavy. The black rose could also represent anyone else out there dealing with difficult stuff.

What do I do when I'm having a hard time? When I feel low or bored and need to think of something peaceful, my mind automatically goes to plants and gardens. That's why there are bright bees, butterflies, dragonflies, wasps, sunflowers, lilies, and snowdrop flowers all around the black rose in the mural. These are my friends and family. I feel better when I imagine myself surrounded by all these different animals and plants, and even better when I'm actually around nature and different people who care about me.

I made *We're All Together* because I hope that if you're like me—someone with a dark sense of humor and who can be somber, or maybe you're facing a hard time—that you remember you always have supporters and a beautiful, peaceful natural world around you to help. As a community, we need to come together and be patient with each other.

As an artist, I usually work in drawing with pencils and pens. Painting, especially something so big, was a new experience for me! There was a lot of trial and error in creating the sketch, projecting it onto the board, and figuring out the logistics to complete it. I want to thank many people: Chyna Edwards and Kailey Bryant-Vaughn for being friends and helping me paint; Sunni Hutton, who let me create the whole piece in her house when I was displaced by the tornado; Dan Beezley, who was my art teacher at Sumner High School and someone I think about every day, for being such a good mentor and friend; CAM staff who encouraged me; and my family, who provided support.

Art, like nature, works best when we're all together.

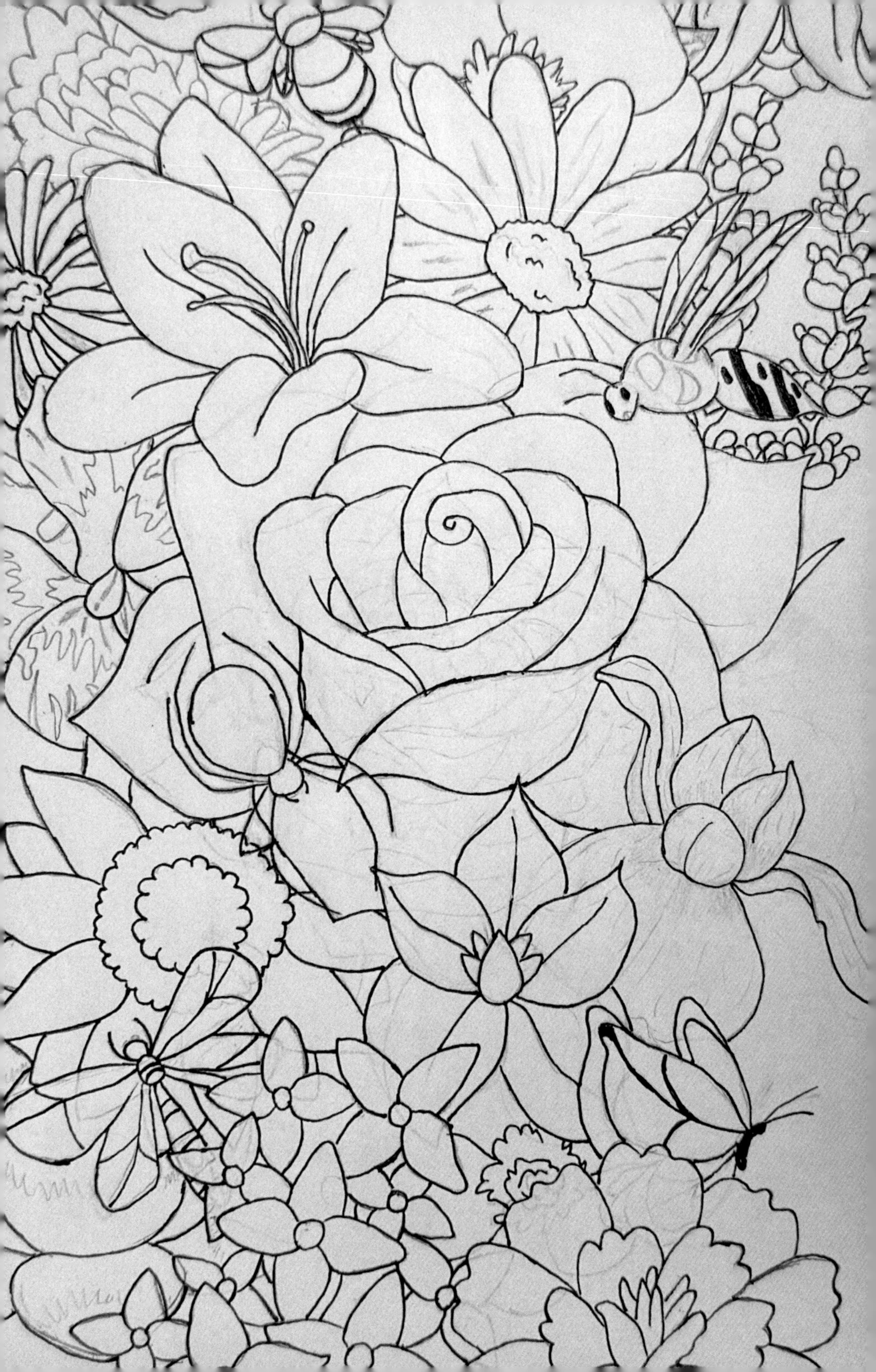

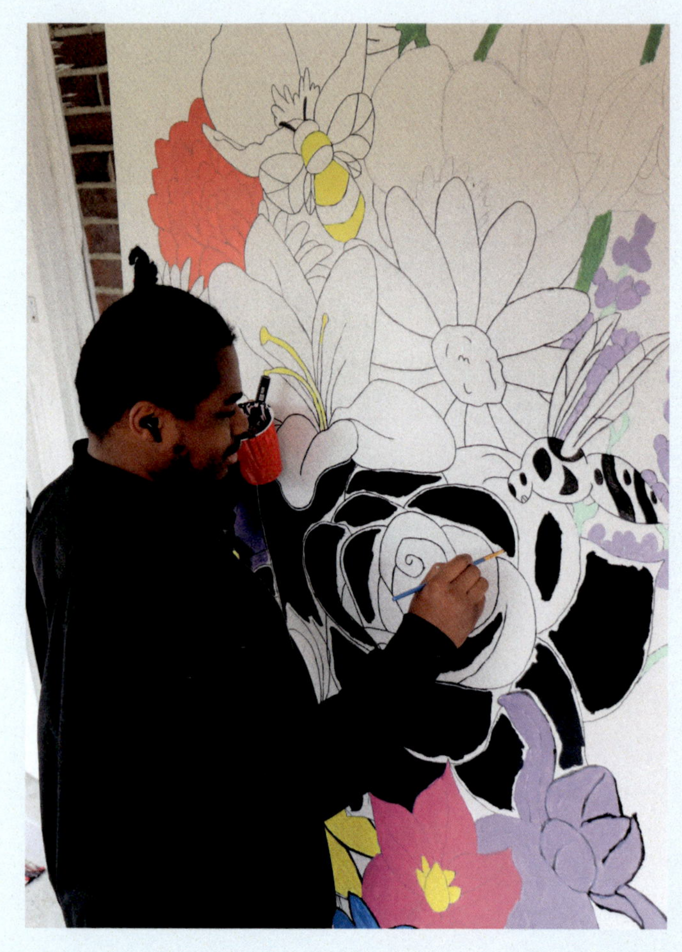

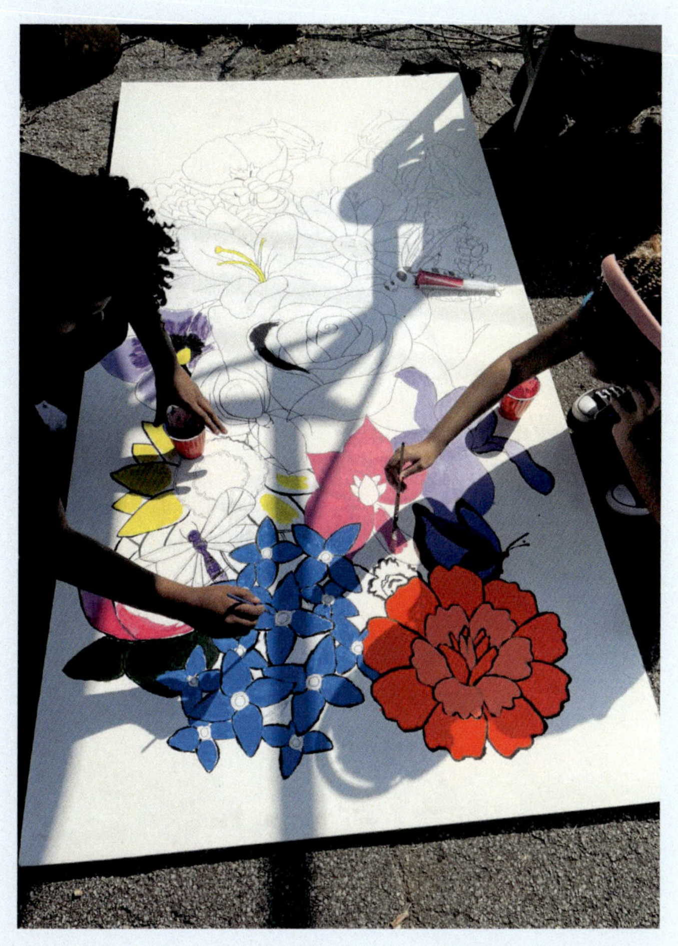

Hidden Currents: From Athlone to O’Fallon Park

Rev. LaQuindlyn Shanae

In North St. Louis, where the Penrose neighborhood now touches O'Fallon Park, a landscape of rolling hills, shaded valleys, and springs once formed the estate of John O' Fallon (1791–1865), one of the city's wealthiest citizens in the mid-nineteenth century. Known as Athlone—a nod to his Irish ancestry—the grounds included orchards, gardens, deer pens, and a columned mansion perched high on a ridge. O'Fallon, nephew of William Clark of the Lewis and Clark Expedition, built his wealth not only through business and philanthropy but also through the forced labor of enslaved people. Today, little physical trace of the Athlone homestead remains. Yet, under the surface stories still flow—of watercourses renamed, of Indigenous and African American lives erased, and of a park landscape that hides as much as it reveals.

The Athlone Estate and Its Waterways

Built in the 1840s, Athlone was O'Fallon's summer home, as he kept a winter residence elsewhere in the city. The mansion, a Greek Revival structure with tall columns, overlooked the Mississippi Bottoms and sat amid carefully laid out carriage drives. Historical sketches show orchards to the south, gardens, and a deer pen for spectacle. When O'Fallon died in 1865, he left the estate to his wife Caroline. In 1875, the city of St. Louis purchased the property to establish O'Fallon Park. Later that year, fire damaged the house, and by 1892 the park commissioner recommended its full removal. Demolition followed soon after, leaving only memories and the name.

Central to the estate's landscape was a shaded valley promenade known as "The Walk." Beneath it flowed a large natural spring that fed into what maps and reminiscences call Ginn Grass (Gingrass, Gingras) Creek. This watercourse ran east and northeast, paralleling Broadway Street before

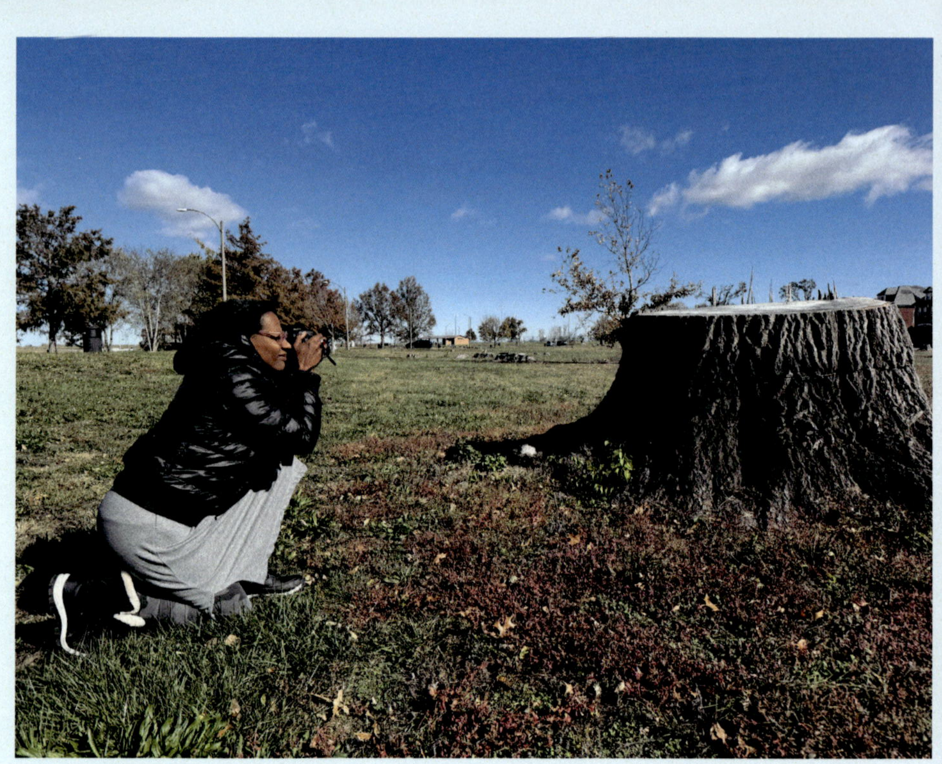

draining into the Mississippi Lowlands. Historic plates clearly show the creek line and the pond it fed, which later became the park's lake. Further downstream, the same body of water appears in Jennings, Missouri, under the name Gingras Creek, now a tributary of Maline Creek. This continuity reveals that the Athlone spring was not just an estate ornament but the headwaters of a regional watershed that still flows today. The spring provided drinking water for local residents and O'Fallon's stables. For the enslaved laborers who maintained the orchards and gardens, it was also a site of daily labor.

Enslavement and Indigenous Presence

While park histories from the 1950s romanticize Athlone as a place of gardens and deer, census records and abolitionist testimonies tell another story: O'Fallon enslaved dozens of African Americans. Estimates suggest he held as many as seventy-seven people across several decades, making him one of the largest slaveholders in St. Louis. In 1856, at least three enslaved people escaped from his estate, joining a larger "stampede" of freedom seekers reported in the press. There are also hints of Indigenous ancestry among those enslaved in St. Louis, though Missouri law officially prohibited slavery of Indigenous people. The recovery of bones, stone axes, and arrowheads near Athlone's cellar during later excavations points to Indigenous presence on the land, likely burial mounds or settlement sites that have been long ignored. Twentieth-century accounts dismissed them as "Stone Age relics," reflecting how archaeology has been used to deny Indigenous history in the region.

From Estate to Park: Memory, Erasure, and Recovery

The city's purchase of Athlone transformed it into a public park. By the 1950s, the pond was stocked with fish, orchards were paved over for tennis courts, and the deer pen gave way to picnic shelters. What had been a plantation powered by enslaved labor was rebranded as a gift to the city from its “benefactor.” Yet, this transformation also buried memory, both physically and symbolically. The spring was piped underground into the sewer. The creek was renamed and fragmented. The enslaved community was erased from commemorative plaques. And the land’s earlier Indigenous presence was ignored.

Public memory is shaped by what communities choose to remember—and deliberately forget. Landscapes hold stories and parks are not neutral ground. To celebrate O’Fallon without acknowledging the people he enslaved continues a legacy of silence. To enjoy the park’s lake without remembering the spring beneath The Walk severs residents from the deeper hydrology of their place. For the Penrose, College Hill, and O’Fallon neighborhoods and broader St. Louis, recovering these hidden currents offers a chance to reimagine how the African American and Indigenous people who plowed the land are commemorated. By following the spring and creek back to their source, we can begin to restore those hidden histories to the landscape.

This article is dedicated to the memory of my grandmother, Mama Dora King.

References

"The 1856 St. Louis Slave Stampede," Slave Stampedes on the Southern Borderlands, Dickinson College, October 9, 2019, https://housedivided.dickinson.edu/sites/stampedes/the-1856-st-louis-stampede/.

Paul Beckwith, *Creoles of St. Louis* (St. Louis: Nixon-Jones Printing Co., 1893).

Wm. S. Bryan and Robert Rose, *A History of the Pioneer Families of Missouri* (St. Louis: Bryan, Brand & Co., 1876).

Richard J. Compton and Camille N. Dry, *Pictorial St. Louis, The Great Metropolis of the Mississippi Valley; A Topographical Survey Drawn in Perspective A.D. 1875*, panoramic map (St. Louis: Compton & Co., 1876).

Encyclopedia of the History of St. Louis, Vol. 3, ed. Howard Louis Conard and William Hyde (St. Louis: Southern History Company, 1899).

"Exodus of Slaves," *St. Louis Globe-Democrat* (St. Louis, MO), July 16, 1856.

Julius Pitzman, *Pitzman's New Atlas of the City and County of Saint Louis, Missouri* (Philadelphia: A. B. Holcombe & Co., 1878).

Sanborn Fire Insurance Maps, St. Louis (1890s–1900s)

"Slave Stampede," *Missouri Republican* (St. Louis, MO), July 16, 1856.

St. Louis Park Department Reports (1875, 1892)

Geoff Ward and Kelly Schmidt, "Remembering John O'Fallon," The Wash U & Slavery Project, Washington University in St. Louis, August 11, 2021, https://slavery.wustl.edu/news/remembering-john-ofallon.

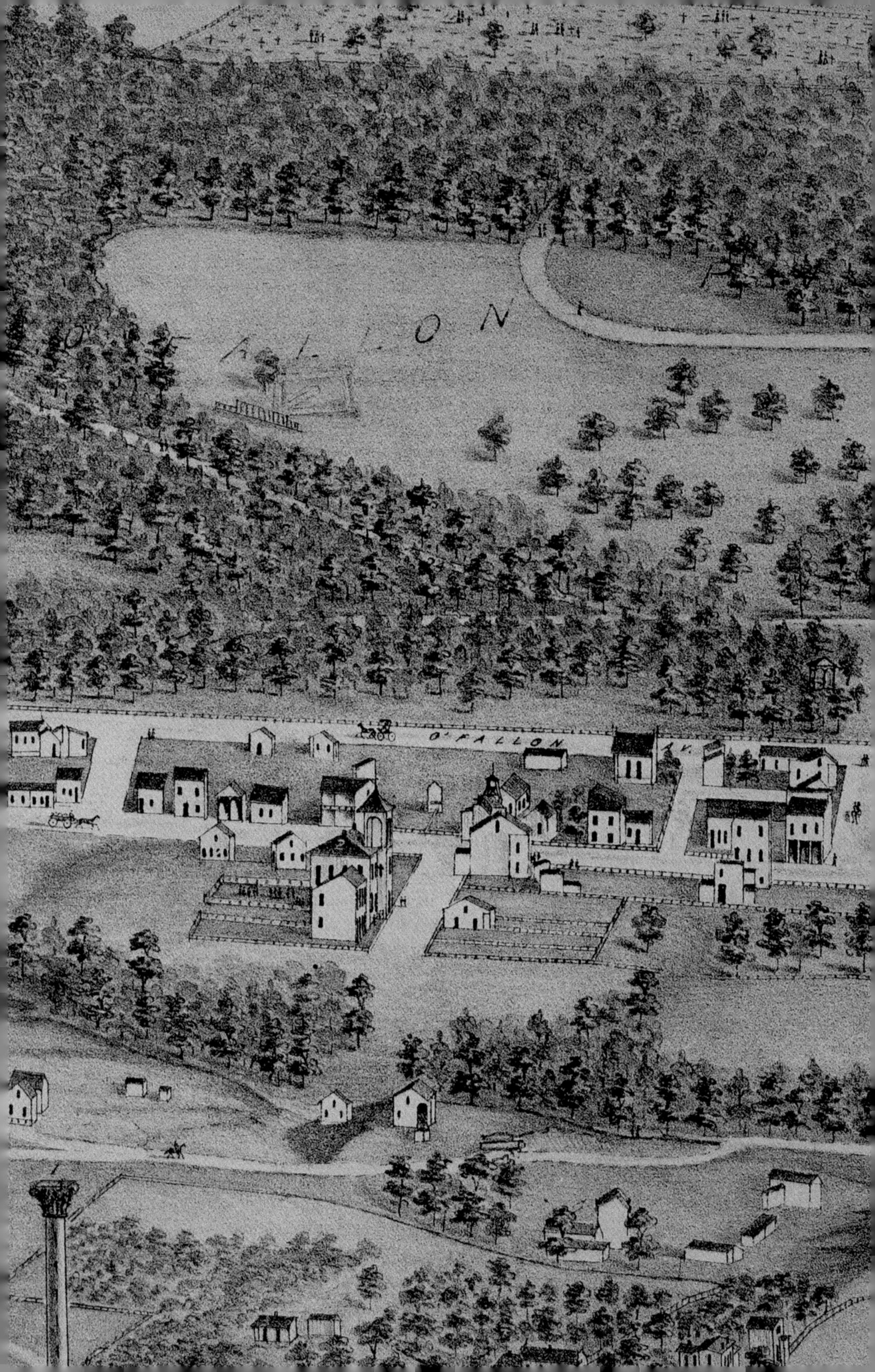
O'FALLON AV.

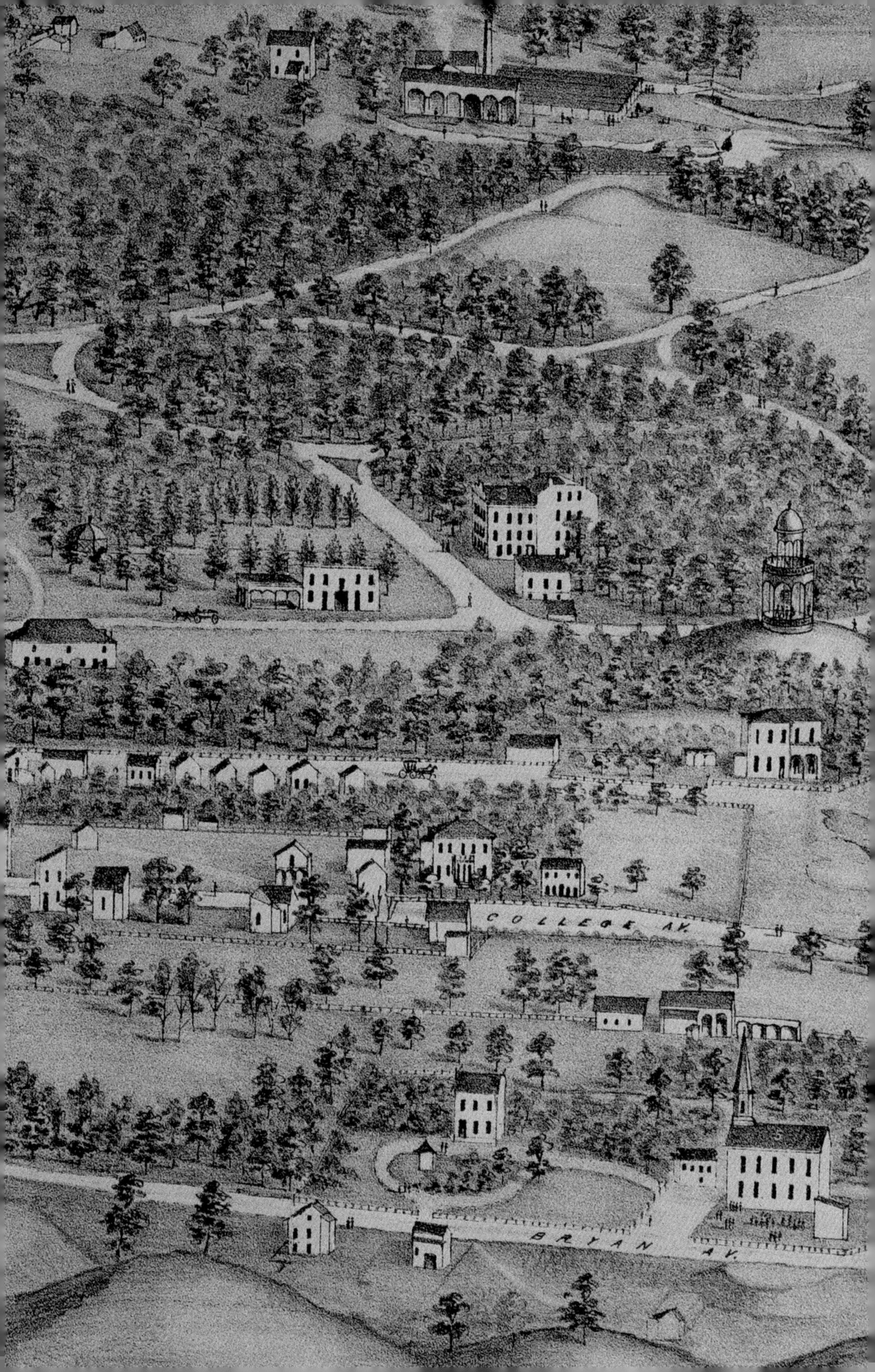
COLLEGE AV.
BRYAN AV.

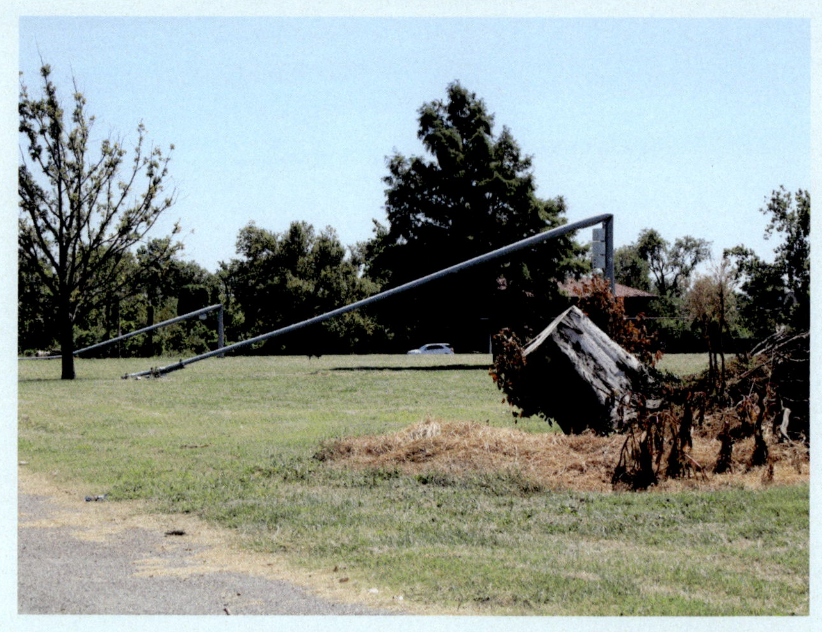

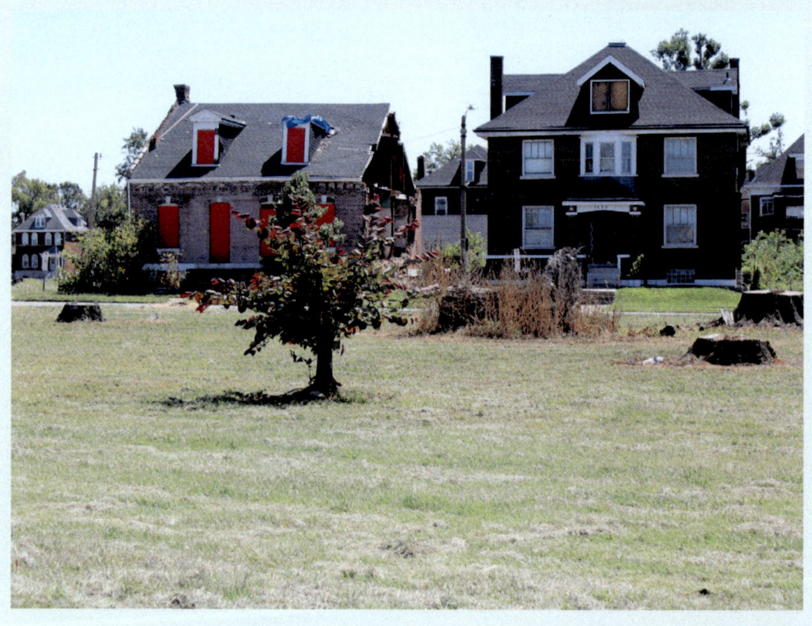

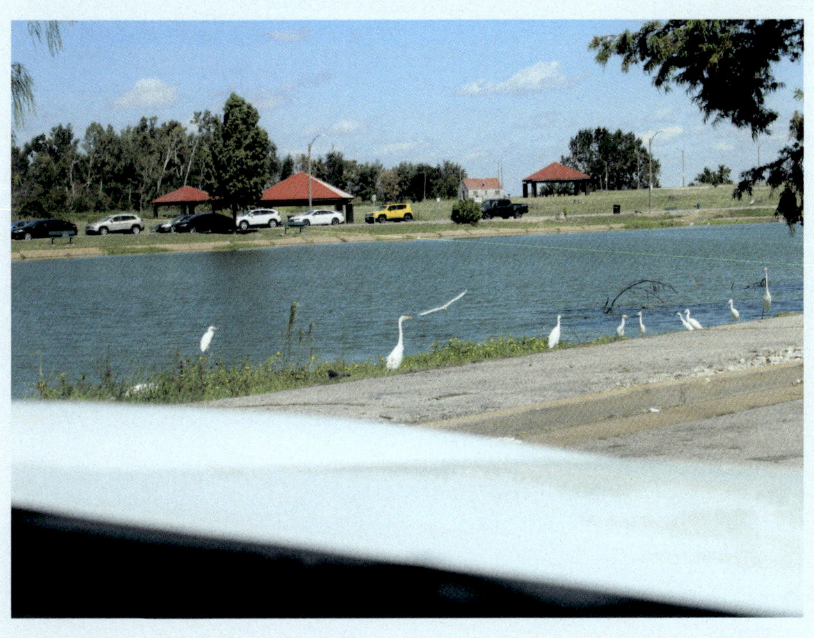

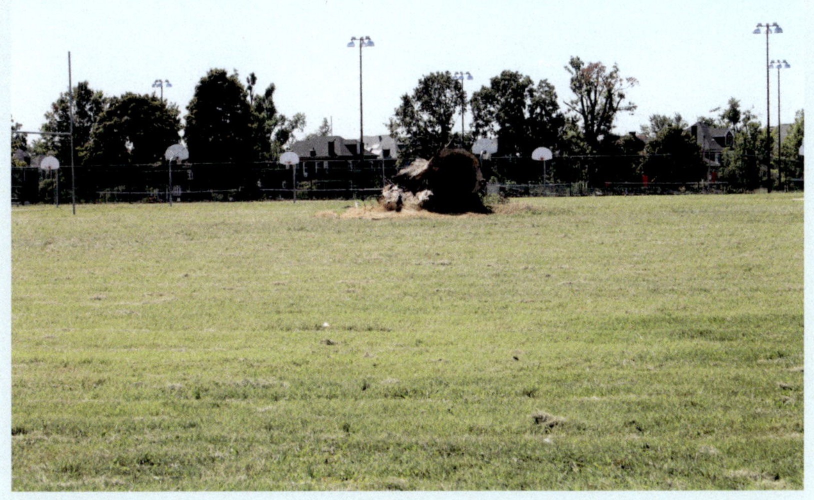

Composting as a Universal Process

Cary Brown

A couple years ago I began spending time at my neighbor's community garden. Before that, I had only grown a mint plant in a pot. It was all very new to me, but also interesting and enjoyable at the same time. Early on, I "got" that an environment that grows tomatoes, peppers, corn, sunflowers, and marigolds will grow lots of other things as well—unwanted things included. So, in the name of making a positive contribution, I locked into mowing, weeding, and cutting back overgrowth. A lot of it.

It was like the land itself had its own massive gardening project and was tireless and unrelenting in going about it. The entire site seemed to encourage, even command: Grow! What it took to try and stay ahead of it was humbling and impressive. There are signs posted around the garden that simply say, "Beautiful. Healthy. Resilient." I had to concede to the truth of that message. Even if the selected plants struggled, countless others flourished in the exact same spot. I could call them weeds or overgrowth if I wanted—but the soil, water, and sun obviously made no such distinction.

Hmmm... soil, water, sun. This isn't new information, but something I got. Like mowing, waiting, and clipping. There was nothing I could do about the amount of sunshine or rain except supplement with water. That left me thinking about supplementing the soil. A bit of looking into fertilizing quickly brought up composting, so I decided to see if I could get something going with an unused compost bin. It's a nice size garden, so there's plenty of stuff around to compost. Someone even began donating lots of old produce.

It didn't take long before things started to happen. Bugs. Worms. Wet it. Flip it. Add greens. Add browns. Repeat.

Repeat. The stuff at the bottom was definitely changing. Breaking down. The compost bin was its own little ecosystem. I had a blast with the process—and I got some nice compost a few times.

In an effort to learn more, I came across a method called "direct composting." It made even more sense to me, so in the fall I dug trenches in a few of the beds and buried scraps of produce and paper, even sardines and tuna. I continued into the spring and saw the bugs and worms proliferate just as they did in the bin. I saw the soil change. I purposefully chose beds with dirt that had the most clay where things might struggle to grow anyway (just in case my experiment didn't work out). I was glad to see I was getting so much better with this process: Darker. Richer. All so naturally.

I thought of forests, plains, jungles, rivers, lakes, and oceans. Even the dirt in the yards, alleys, and lots in my North St. Louis neighborhood. Erosion breaking down rock. Releasing minerals. Minerals feeding tiny things. Tiny things feeding larger things. All living things dying, decomposing, and adding ingredients back into the mix.

I like thinking about how it all started eons ago. Helium and hydrogen clumping together, forming stars that squeeze and cook into other elements. Stars exploding and blasting their new contents across space. New stars forming, but seeded with more ingredients than before. Unused stuff condensing into planets around them. Planets taking in the energy spewing forth from the fusion. It's like how the Earth and the Sun support the growth and development of a myriad of living things here that go on to fold into the continual breakdown and consumption of things.
It's such a staggeringly large and ancient process.

I’ve come to really appreciate my garden experience and how it has introduced me to thinking about the deeply rooted recycling process that takes place cosmically—and also in a garden and a plot of land in North St. Louis. I see a lot clearer now, of course ... grow!

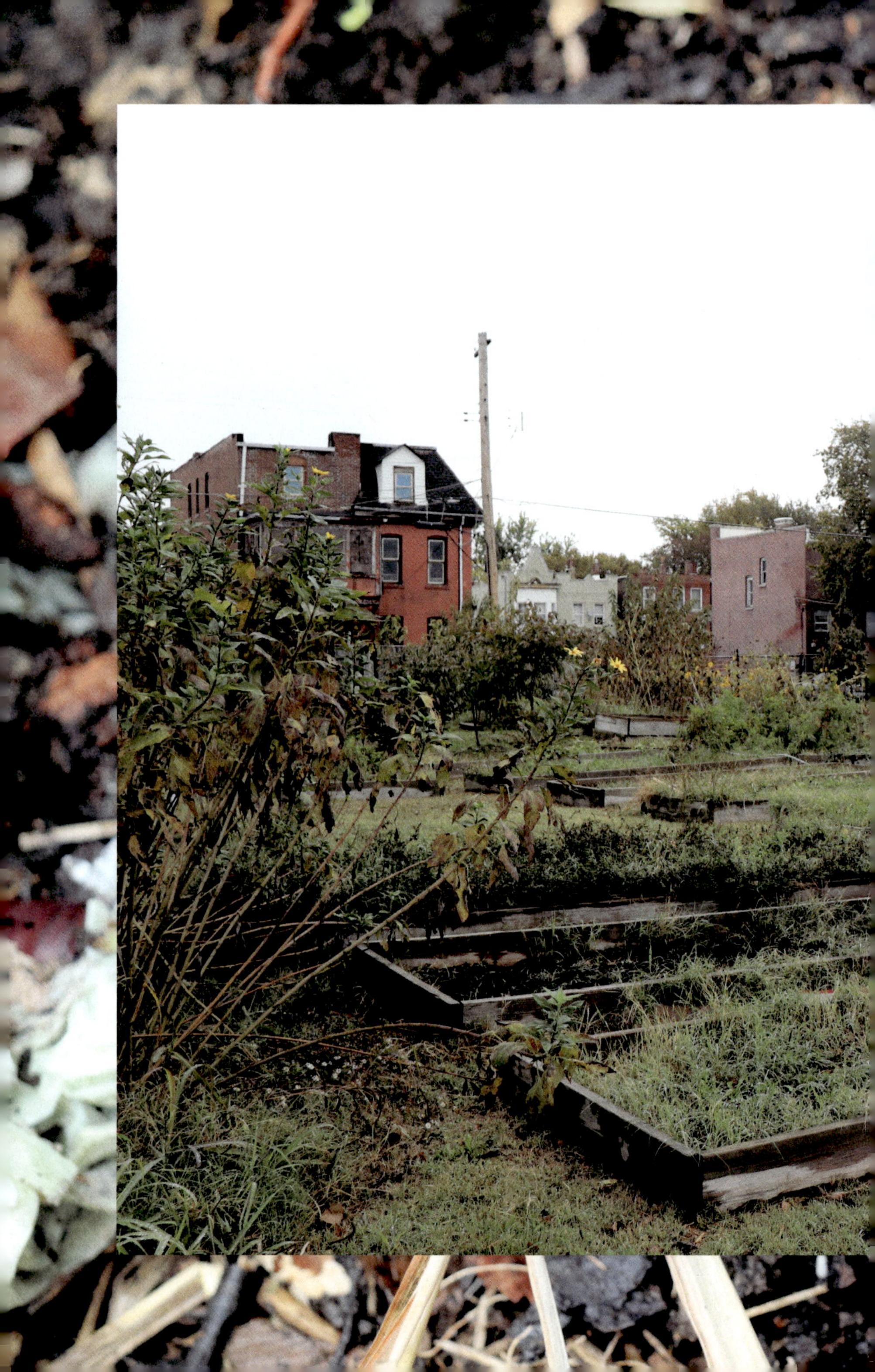

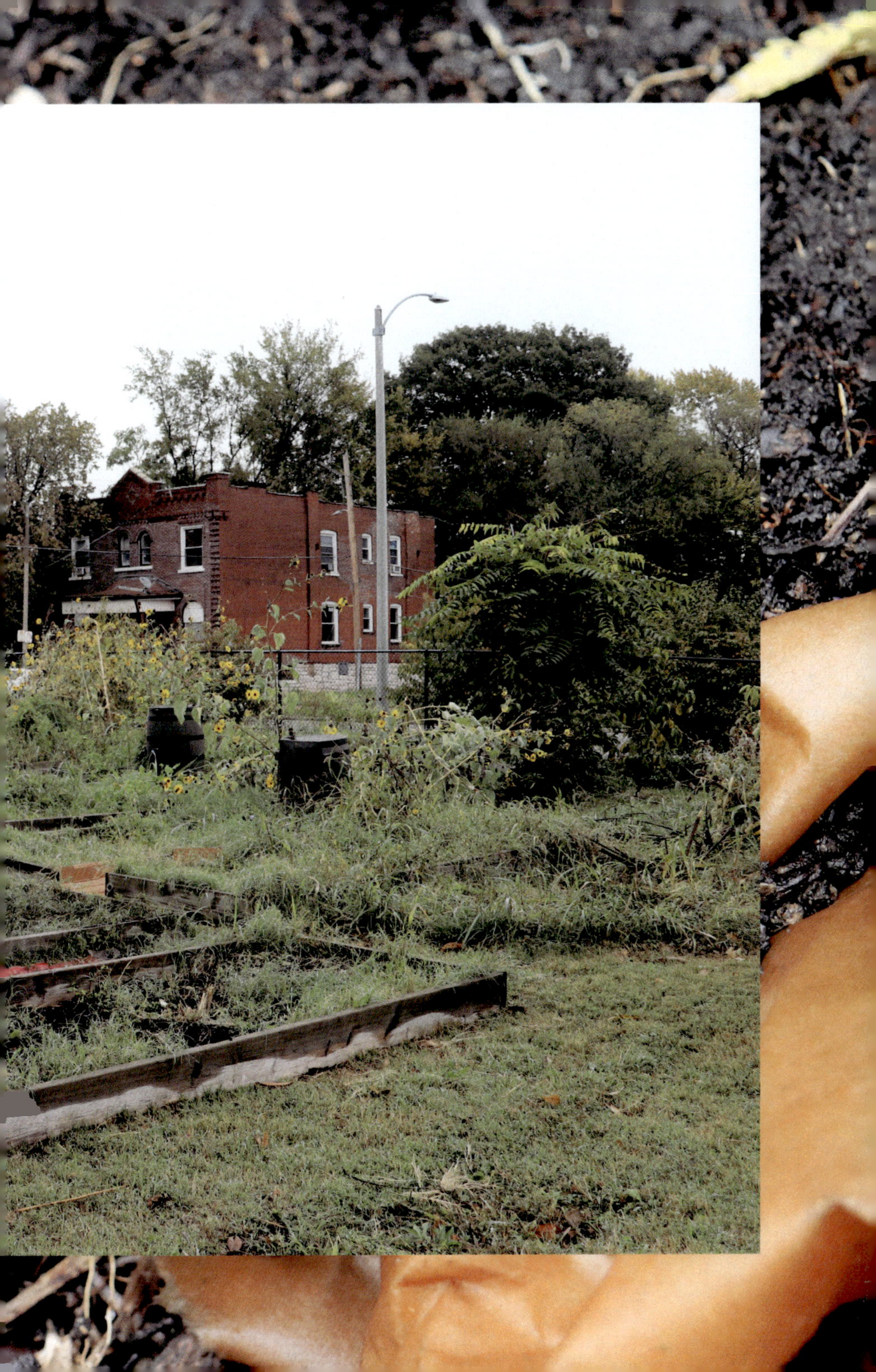

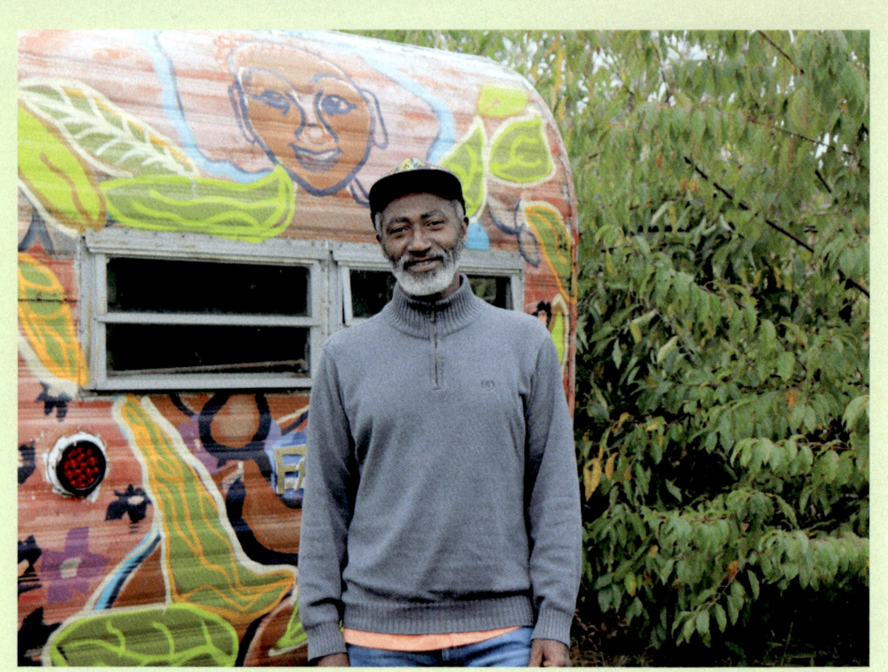

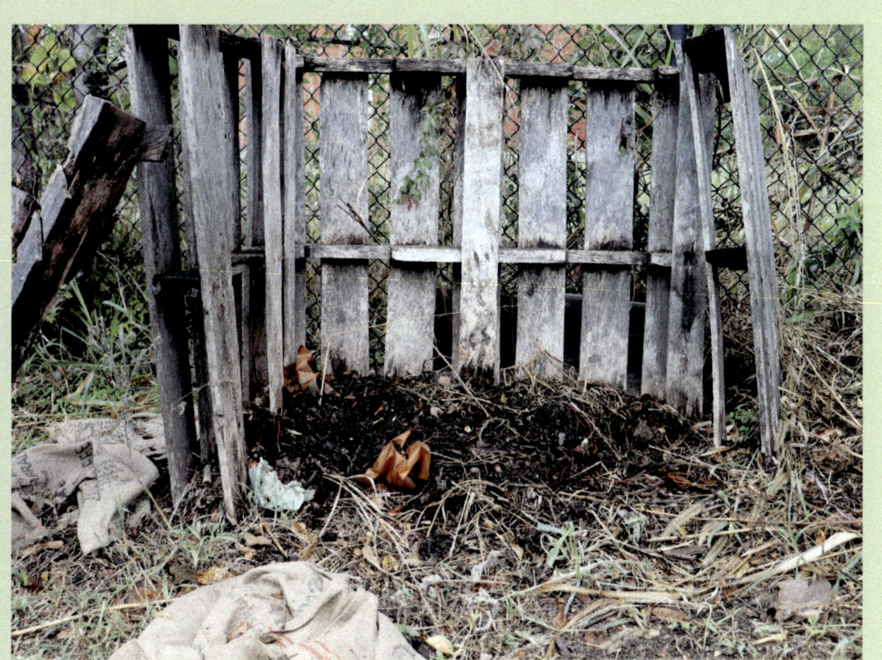

Cultivating Sacred Movement Through Mind, Body, and Soul

Ronda Smith Branch

When asked about my art, I smile. There is no easel, no canvas. My studio? It's everywhere my feet touch the earth, every place I can tend and be tended to. It happens every time I open my heart to use my movement to tell you a story. My garden dissolves boundaries entirely, allowing wherever I cultivate to become my canvas, my tools, and my sanctuary—all at once.

Movement isn't just labor when you're working your land. It's how you connect, how you heal, how you *truly* feel a space. This isn't your typical choreography—this is storytelling with your whole being, communing with Source energy through the same cycles that teach a flower when to bloom and when to rest.

I work with what I call sacred movement: the intentional cultivation of mind, body, and soul through every plane of our existence. Sexual, material, emotional, intellectual, spiritual—using all our senses to honor how we show up as physical manifestations of something much bigger than ourselves.

Here's how it breaks down:

Mind of the mind, Body of the mind, Soul of the mind
Mind of the body, Body of the body, Soul of the body
Mind of the soul, Body of the soul, Soul of the soul

A trinity within a trinity. This framework has birthed an internal evolutionary wisdom: "Know with your heart, trust through the body, do from the soul," in which each intersection teaches you something different. Mind movements dig into history and plant insights in the present moment. Body movements build practical resilience—learning to bend without breaking, standing strong when it matters, protecting what's tender. Soul movements transform ordinary living into sacred practice, working with cycles of growth, decay, and renewal that make your garden itself part of the art.

This work centers Black, Brown, and Indigenous women because we're the ones leading rematriation—restoring sacred relationships between our people and ancestral land, honoring our matrilineal societies. The garden studio becomes a place where we reclaim both identity and connection to place.

What emerges is what I call a *Sankofa* life practice that intentionally draws on the past to inform the present and future—deeply rooted, resilient, adaptable. It protects and nurtures growth across all our ages and stages. This positions the work within broader conversations about healing that serve both individual transformation and collective liberation.

Through integrating sacred movement with my personal garden spaces, my studio expands into a living installation that feeds both me and my community. It's an artistic practice that holds ancient wisdom and contemporary application in the same hands.

Go find where your own personal garden studio space is waiting—it's wherever your feet can touch earth and your spirit can tend to what needs tending.

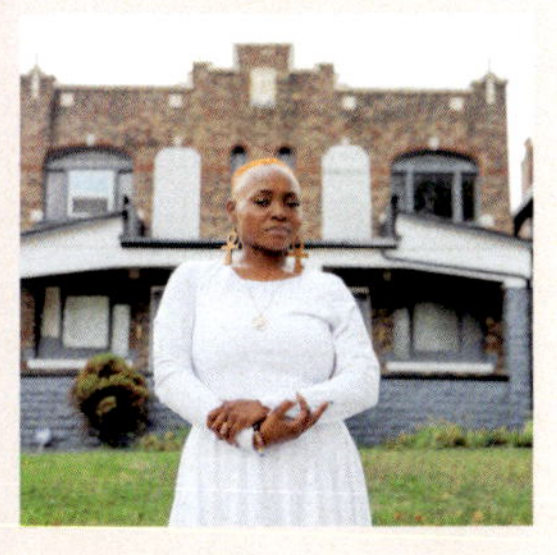
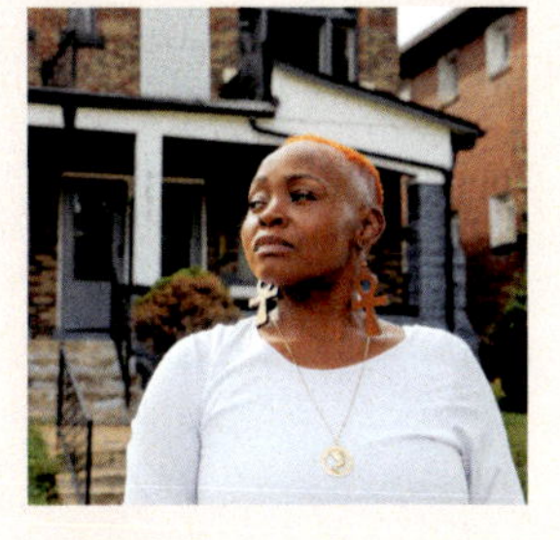
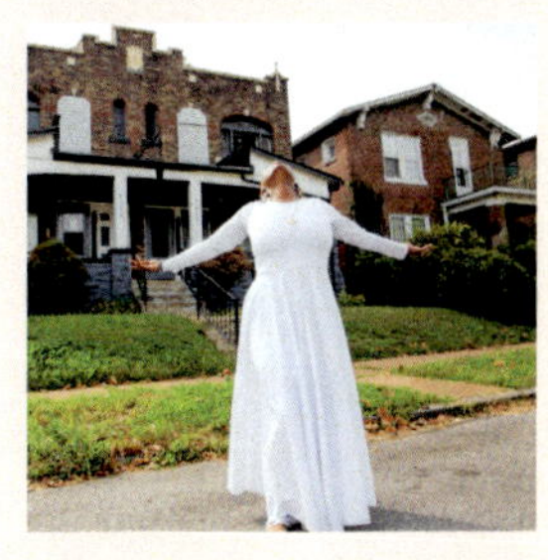
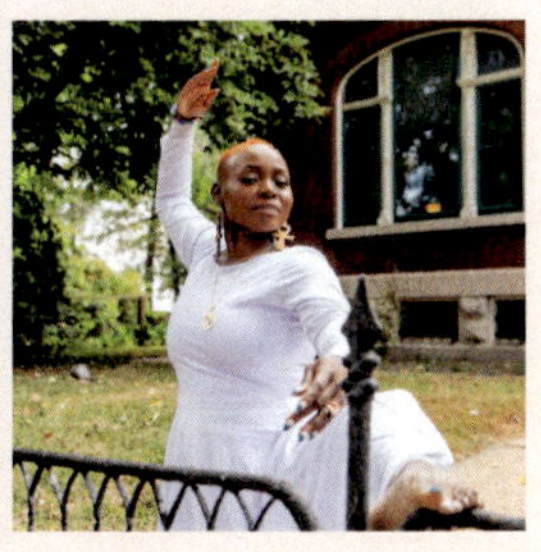
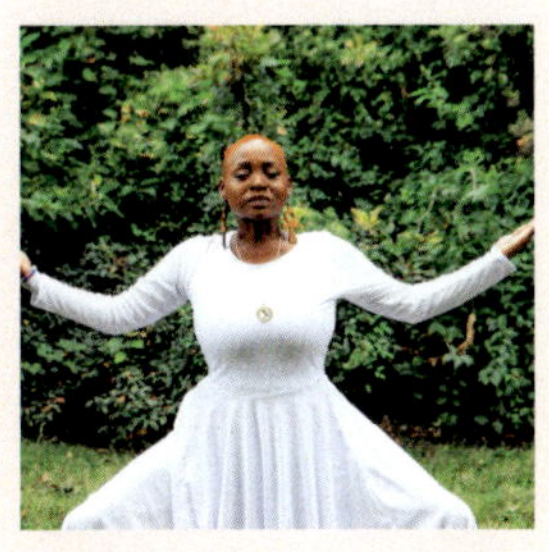
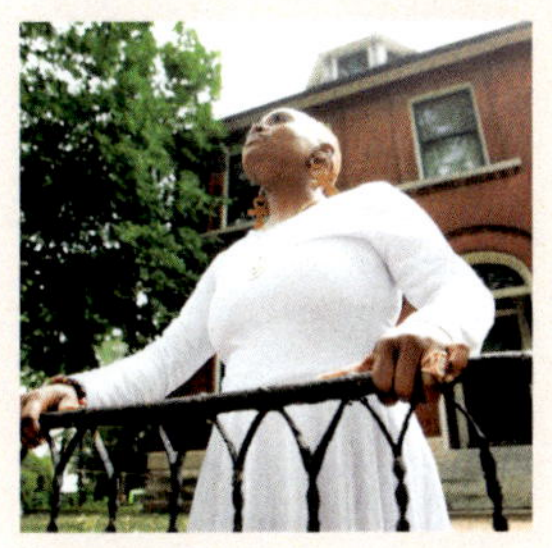
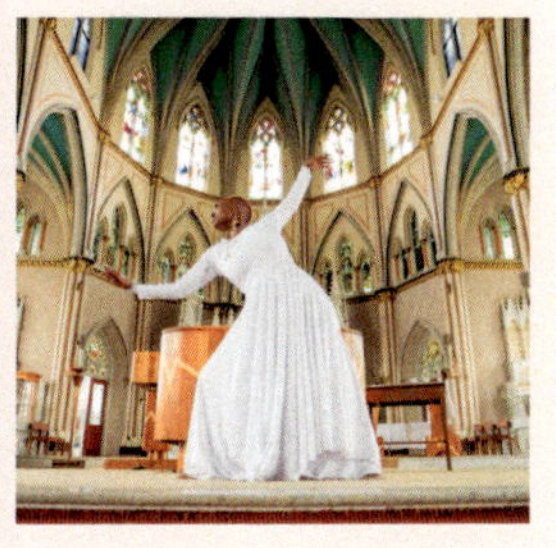
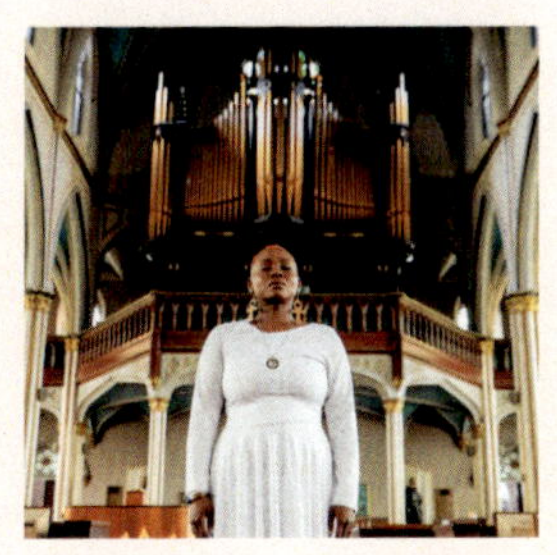
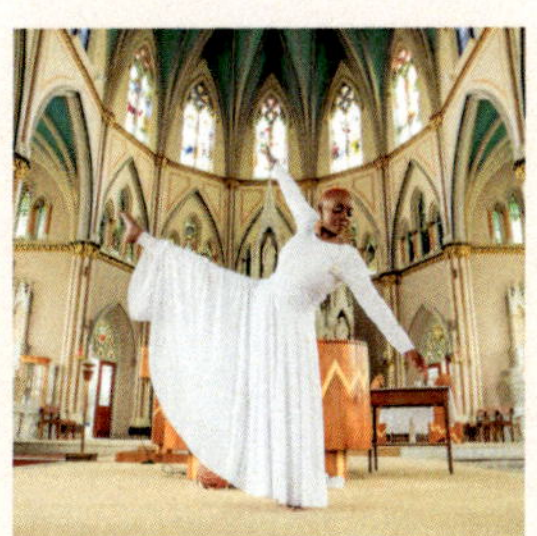

Growing in Chaos: Rainbow Resilience Bed

Gabi Cole

For the past decade, the Fit and Food Connection has stood as a source of nourishment, wellness, and healing in North St. Louis. Fit and Food, which I co-founded in 2015, was born from the belief that access to healthy food and wellness practices is a right, not a privilege, for my fellow residents of North St. Louis City. What began as a grassroots vision to deliver fresh produce and accessible programs has grown into a movement that connects thousands of neighbors each year to resources that affirm their health, dignity, and future.

From the earliest community gardens to our Healthy Food Pantry to the Mobile Meals program, Fit and Food has worked side by side with residents to reimagine what is possible when access meets love and commitment. Food here is more than sustenance: it is medicine, it is memory, it is culture, and it is community power. Over the years, we've witnessed not only the growth of plants and programs, but the growth of people: neighbors who find strength in yoga, parents who bring their children to volunteer in the garden, families who gather around fresh produce.

As we mark the milestone of ten years supporting our community, we also honor the land that has held both struggle and resilience. North St. Louis bears the visible scars of disinvestment: vacant lots, abandoned homes, and systems that too often overlook the people who remain. Yet, it is within this very soil that new life emerges.

Our latest garden installation, *Growing in Chaos: Fit and Food's Rainbow Resilience Bed* (2025), is both a physical and symbolic expression of that truth. The *Rainbow Resilience Bed* is a flower garden designed in radiant layers of color, each tied to the chakras, symbols of energy, healing, and wholeness. Each bloom in the bed carries a story. Red roots of survival. Orange blossoms of creativity. Yellow rays of power and determination. Green leaves of compassion. Blue petals of truth and voice. Indigo stems of wisdom. Violet crowns of spirit.

Where others might see only vacancy, this garden celebrates the presence of neighbors who refused to leave, leaders who chose to invest time and care, and a community that continues to center itself despite the chaos around it. Together we create a living rainbow, an ongoing reminder that growth and healing are not abstract ideals, but rather daily practices nurtured in community.

The *Rainbow Resilience Bed* honors what North St. Louis has always known: that beauty, strength, and healing can rise, even from fractured ground. As Fit and Food looks ahead to the next decade, we remain guided by this lesson. Amid disinvestment, we choose cultivation. Amid vacancy, we choose abundance. Amid chaos, we choose to grow, together.

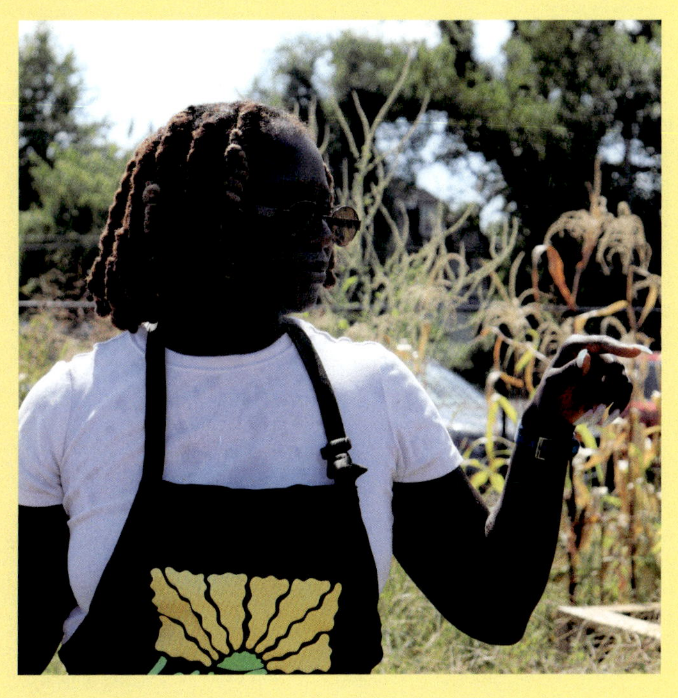

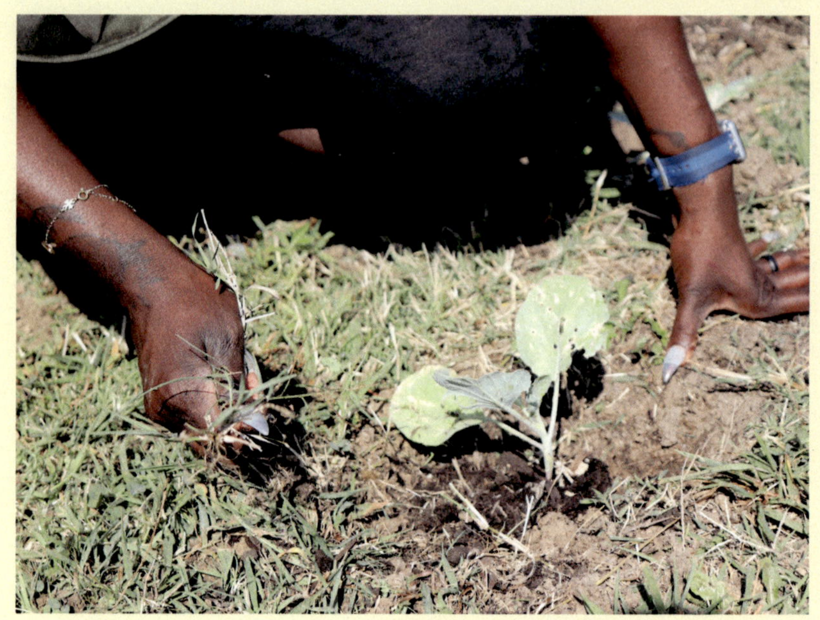

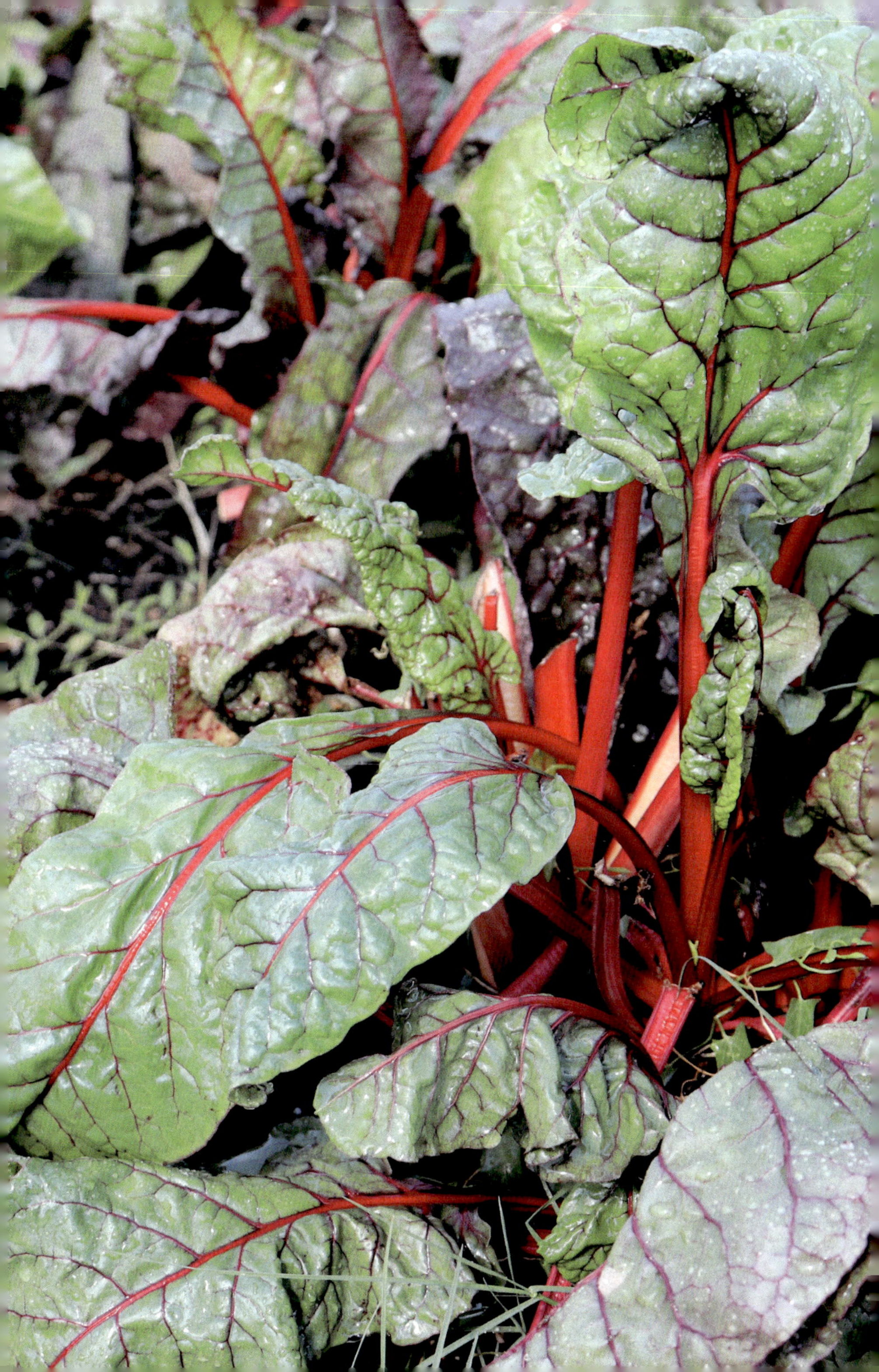

Seeds for the Future: A.C.R.E.S.

Tosha Phonix

As a lifelong North St. Louis resident, my roots run deep in the community that has shaped who I am and what I create. I am the founder and executive director of A.C.R.E.S. (Agriculture for Community Restoration, Economic Justice & Sustainability), an organization born from the unwavering belief that our community holds within it all the power, wisdom, and resources needed to flourish. Dedicated to empowering Black farmers and communities, A.C.R.E.S. strives to cultivate a culture of self-determination over their food system and built environment.

Since 2011, I have been growing sustainable produce throughout North St. Louis City and County. In 2025, we finished developing a quarter-acre farm in Walnut Park on what was once a vacant lot. This garden represents far more than agriculture. By addressing the historical and ongoing discrimination faced by Black farmers and underserved communities, A.C.R.E.S. amplifies their voices in shaping a more just and inclusive food system.

My work is deeply influenced by my faith and the teachings of self-determination in the Nation of Islam. The Quran guides us to take responsibility for the care and stewardship of the environment, and that humans are not above nature, but rather intrinsically connected with it. Surah 40 teaches that, “The creation of the heavens and earth is greater than the creation of mankind, but most of the people do not know.” I appreciate how this shows up in the long history of Islamic gardens—spaces where people exist in harmony with nature and water plays a central role in bringing purification, nourishment, balance, and peace. The large water feature in our Walnut Park farm and my approach reflects this philosophy.

North St. Louis means everything to me, and I love my people here. Our relationships are all about reciprocity. Even though I'm called to a service role, the people don't need me to serve them. We have everything we need in the community. I can play a part to help ensure our resources and mutual aid systems remain strong and stay within our neighborhood.

This farm, this organization, this work—it all springs from love. Love for my neighbors, love for this earth we share, and love for the future we are building together: one seed, one relationship, one season at a time.

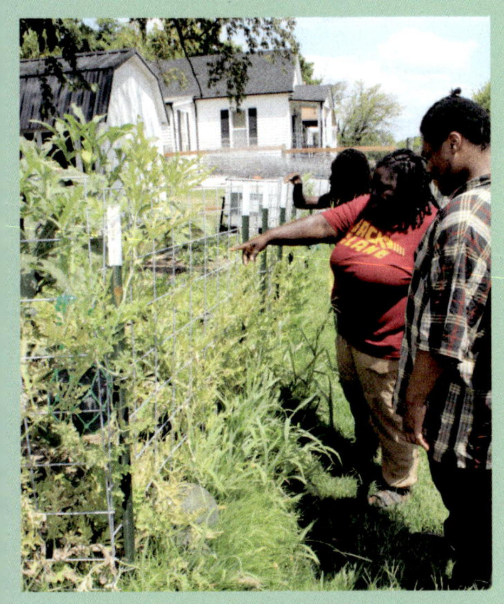

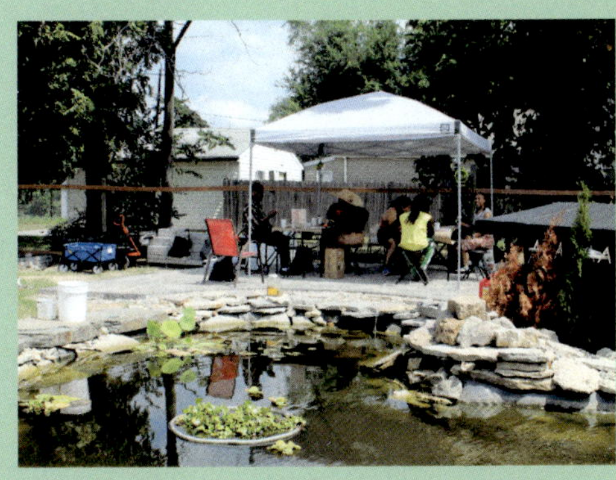

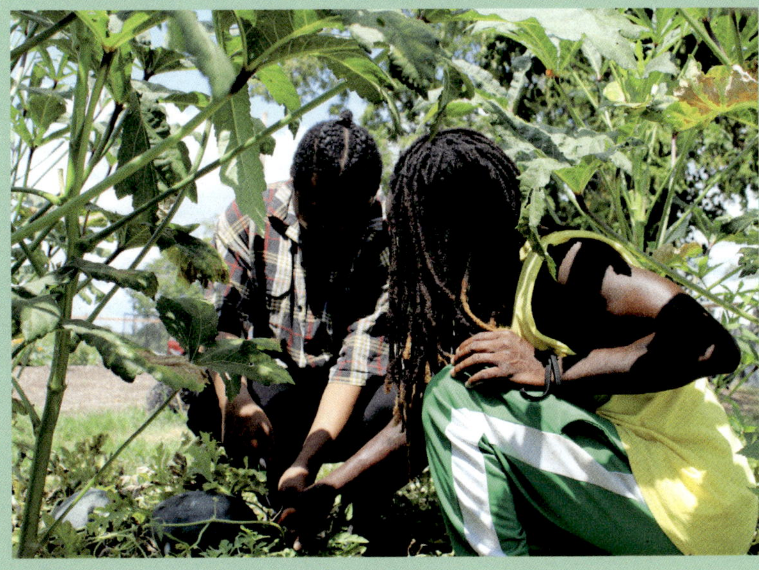

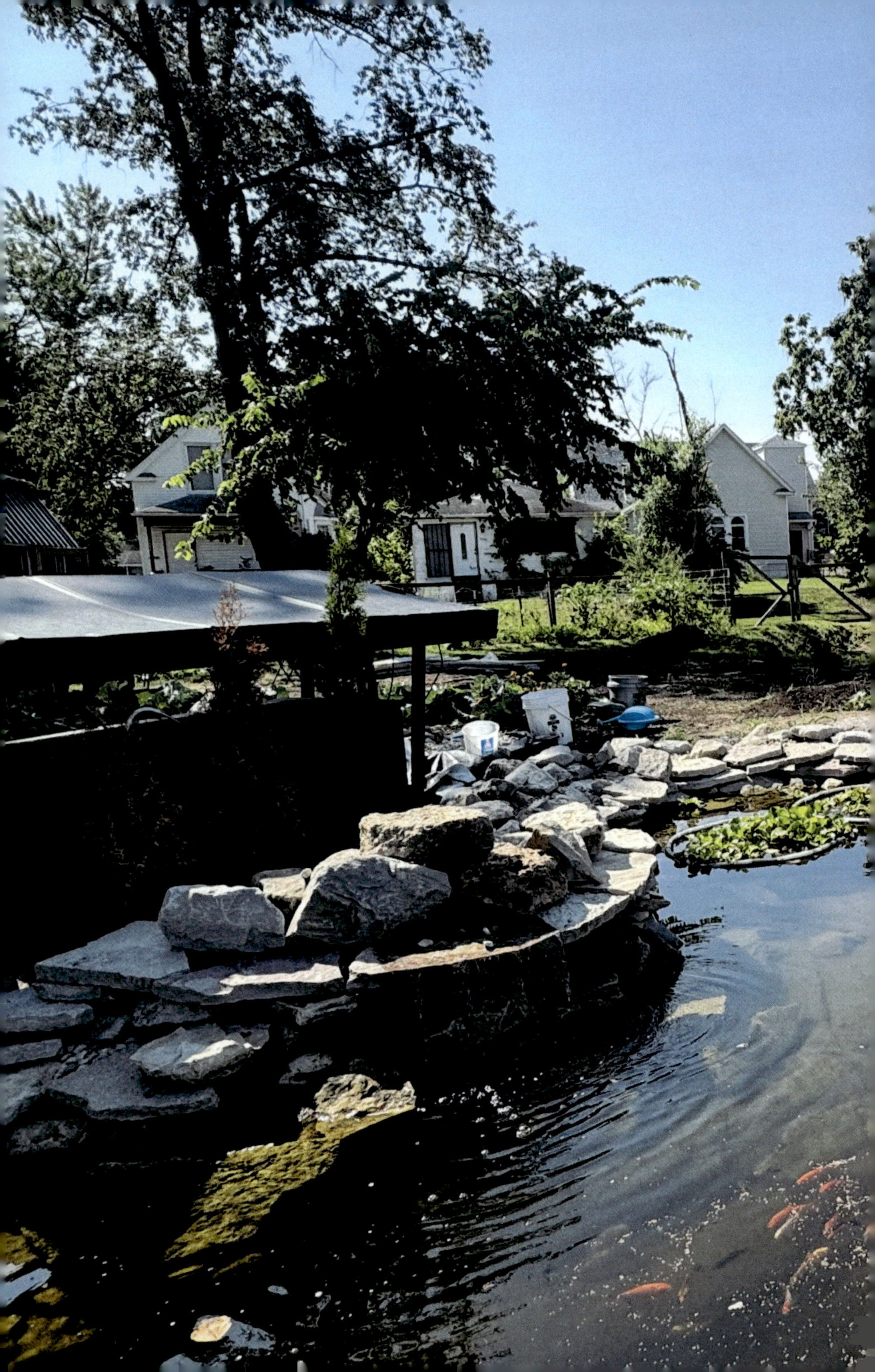

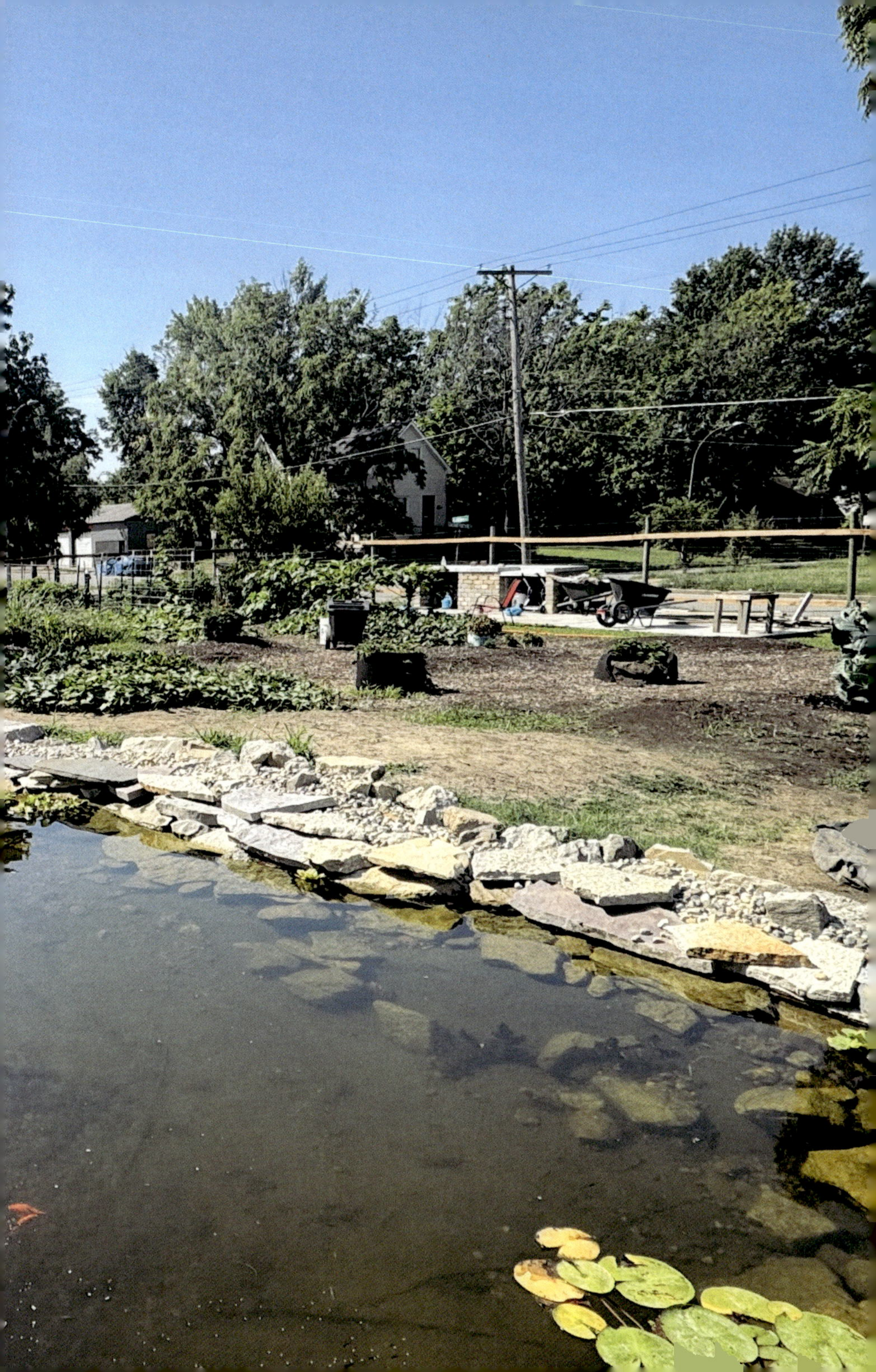

When We Engage with Green Spaces Around Us, Maybe We Find...

Alexis Creamer

As a steward of care, community, and creativity, my practice lives in harmony with deeply impactful memories. Guided by holistic healing, I lean into teachings that bring me closest to self-expression and presence. I work through what's in my mind with my hands and body. Storytelling, movement, and collective creation inform how I show up as a cultural worker and Community Access Manager at CAM.

My history is rooted here in St. Louis. My grandmother, a mother to nine and second-generation immigrant, raising children on North 16th Street and Cass Avenue. I grew up in the Timber Ridge Apartments in Spanish Lake, where green lay between parking lot cracks and a grassy area dipped behind tall tan brick buildings. Treetops towered over our apartment, and branches and leaves tangled themselves in the electricity lines flying adjacent to my mom's bedroom window.

Outside was where I wanted to be. My earliest memory: falling knees first in mud in a new all-pink outfit. When the stains were too much, my mom called on my Aunt Suzanne on Bayonne Drive. Her backyard, which was about three acres wide, had lush green grass that softly lay at the backs of our heels, holding us there as we sat on the patio.

There is privilege in being in nature. A free camp in seventh grade grew my access to green spaces. I was the first of my neighbors to sleep in a tent, lay my body in grass, stargaze without artificial light, identify insects, and run in fields with no end. The ability to ground myself, to pay attention to my surroundings, stayed with me. It reminds me to ask myself: What is in front of me right now? What am I experiencing in the present moment?

When we meet this type of presence, our minds open to imagine, dream, and create. Nature offers us a place to be whole, aware, and connected. In those spaces, we unlock new pathways. When we need a mental break, maybe we might step outside instead of picking up our phones—in doing so, perhaps we'll notice a bushel of native flowers or find a community event.

Maybe we create moments of connection by choosing to be in and a part of what surrounds us. Maybe there is some sense of discovery for you here.

Because of what green spaces are and the power they hold for us, how can we be intentional when we're in them? On the following pages, there are three series of prompts you can follow to help ground yourself in nature.

Intentions

Making an agreement with yourself to act, be, or acquire something is to set an intention.

Self
First, identify what you know now.

What am I aware of in the present moment?

Internal
Next, identify what you intend for your internal self.

What do I want to see, feel, understand, and/or experience through my personal lens?

External

Then, identify how you will manifest this externally.

How will what is inside me show up outside? How will I express this intention?

Lastly, identify what you need to do to be accountable for this agreement.

How will I stay true to what I want to create?

Write and create your intentions here:

Memories

Recall your earliest memory in a green space. Once you've sat in that memory, shift your attention to where you are now.

Be present. Engage all of your senses.

What is around you?

Breathe.

What do you feel?

Breathe.

Remember this new memory in a green space.
Write and create your memories here:

Observations

When you're in a green space, choose something to observe that you feel is worth paying close attention to. It might be a plant, an animal, or something human-made.

Name of observation:

Date:

Time:

Location:

Create a drawing and/or description with as much detail as possible:

Record what you most want to remember about this experience of observation:

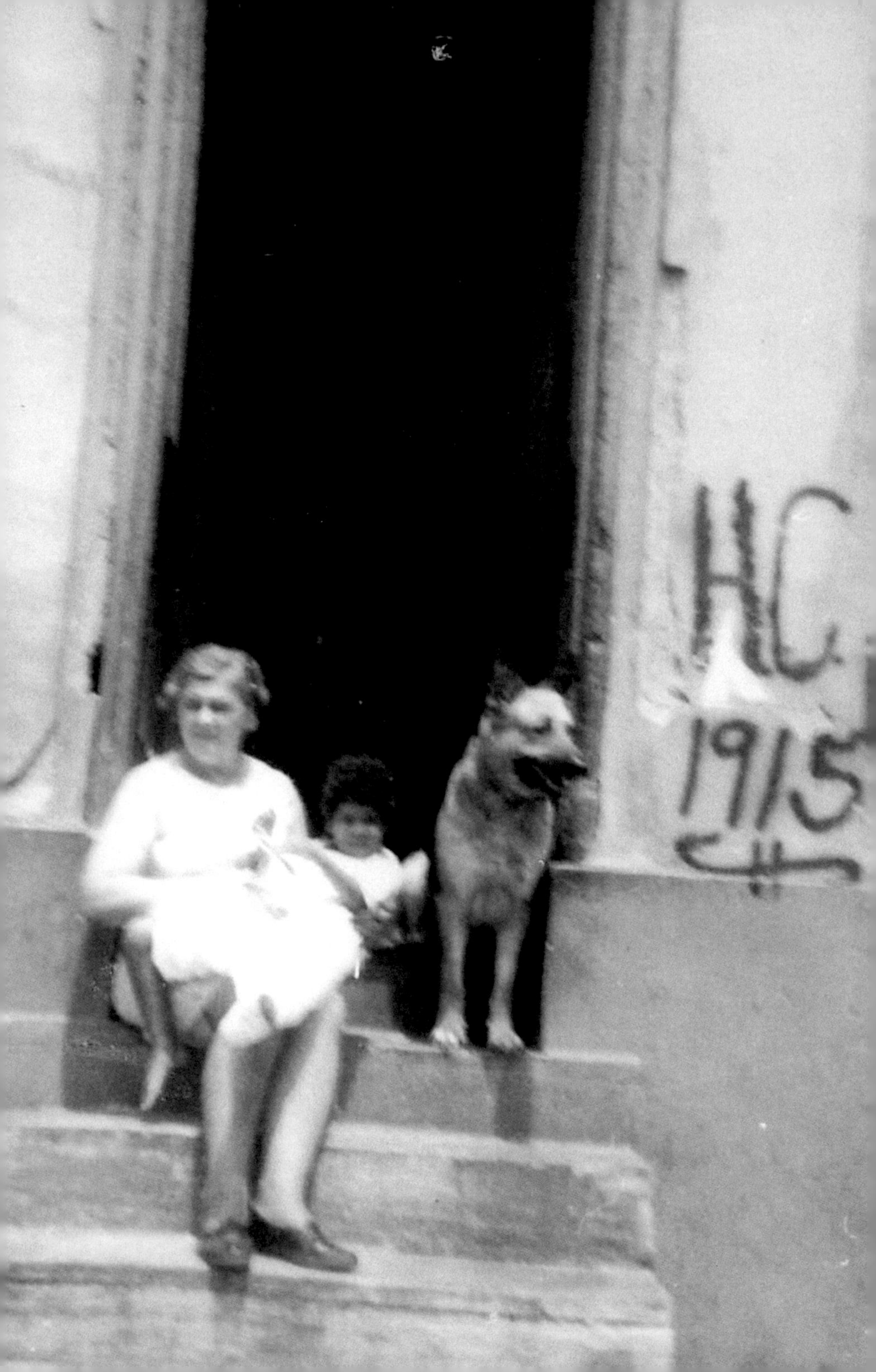
HC
1915

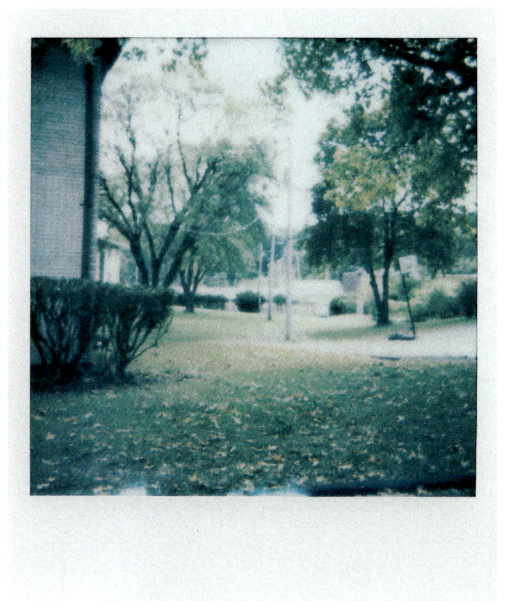

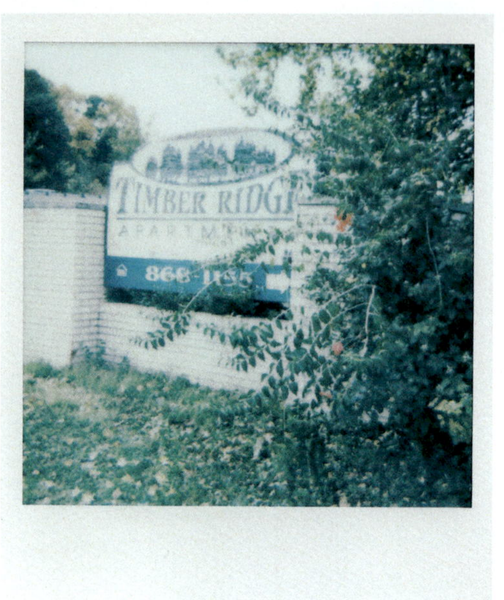
TIMBER RIDG
APARTM

AN ORIGINAL POLAROID® LAND PHOTOGRAPH

SUBJECT ______ DATE 4-1-75

NAME Mrs. Helen Creamer

ADDRESS 1618 N. 16th St.
St. Louis, Mo.

REGULAR SIZE COPIES	
WALLET SIZE COPIES	
5 x 7 ENLARGEMENTS	
8 x 10 ENLARGEMENTS	
35mm SLIDES	

For your convenience when ordering copies, indicate the number of copies desired in the appropriate box for the size(s) you select. You can get quality work by Polaroid Copy Service through your dealer or by mail.

P5588-1 4/72

Printed in U.S.A.

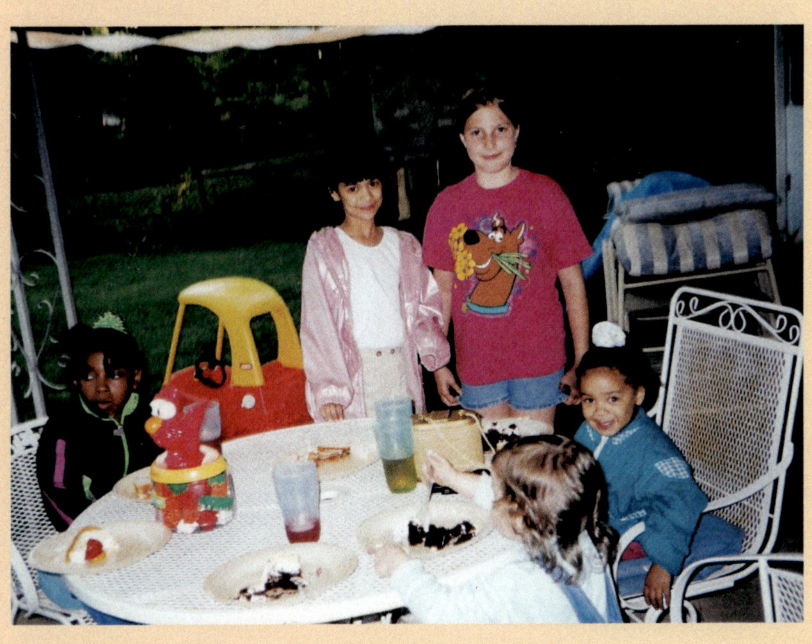

Contributor Biographies

Cary Brown is a father and a musician born and raised in Chicago to a Mississippi-rooted family steeped in church tradition. As a child, he grew his love for reading and comics, developing a passion for drawing that translated into sketching and loving nature—taking perhaps more interest in bugs than humans. He moved to St. Louis as a working musician creating and performing reggae music. He met Dail Chambers through the neighborhood and supports her work in Coahoma Orchards.

Dail Chambers embodies sustainable living through visual and conceptual art. Her community art/agricultural studio and public health campaigns are rooted in storytelling and inspired by Harriet Tubman, Ella Baker, Ntozake Shange, and contemporary rematriating artists. As a land steward, Chambers focuses on public health, environment, and collective memory through archiving, found objects, and ecological/food production that honors migration, culture, and folklore. She creates preventative healthcare support for urban environments. Chambers is a fine artist, mother, caregiver, scholar, educator, and neighbor emphasizing healing practices and ancestral veneration. She is also a seedkeeper, waterkeeper, and personal items appraiser.

Juan William Chávez is a 2012 Guggenheim Fellow in Fine Arts, artist, activist, educator, and beekeeper of Indigenous Latinx and Irish descent. Chávez collaborates on social practice art projects focused on community building, food sovereignty, environmental stewardship, and decolonization. His creative practice includes public art, installations, knowledge-sharing workshops, paintings, zines, unconventional forms of beekeeping, and agriculture. His work was featured in La Trienal 20/21 at El Museo del Barrio and the Counterpublic 2023 triennial, and he has exhibited in venues such as 601Artspace, ArtPace, Tube Factory Artspace, John Michael Kohler Arts Center, and CAM St. Louis. He has received awards from Bloomberg Philanthropies Public Art Challenge, Creative Capital, ArtPlace America, Andy Warhol Foundation for the Visual Arts, and Art Matters.

Gabi Cole, Executive Director and Co-Founder of the Fit and Food Connection, is a North St. Louis native dedicated to equitable wellness and food access. Since establishing her nonprofit in 2012, she's served underserved families through community-led programming. As a consultant, educator, and author, Cole specializes in racial equity work, social justice training, and grassroots organizational development. Her expertise spans community engagement, public relations, and liberatory resource development. A member of the American Public Health Association, she's received numerous leadership and fundraising awards. Cole believes organizations must remain mission-driven and values-centered. She lives in North St. Louis City with her husband and two children.

Alexis Creamer is a St. Louis native and interdisciplinary creative dedicated to creative expression, and community building. Through mind-body awareness, storytelling, and co-creation, Creamer cultivates spaces that center connection and shared abundance. She currently serves as Community Access Manager at CAM St. Louis and is an active community member, serving on the junior board of The Luminary and the community advisory boards of the Black Genome Project and Fit and Food Connection. Rooted in her lineage as the daughter of a Deaf and disabled individual, Creamer's work bridges art, wellness, and advocacy. Her practice and leadership emphasize the power of collective creativity and accessible pathways toward social and holistic well-being.

Michelle Dezember is an arts educator and programmer with twenty years of experience in museums and communities across the United States, Spain, and Qatar. As Director of Learning and Engagement at CAM, she builds relationships with artists, cultural stewards, and community members to create meaningful public engagement and partnerships. She serves on the Sumner High School Advisory Board and as a peer reviewer for the *Journal of Museum Education*. Having lived in diverse landscapes—deserts, mountains, oceansides, and cities—she is passionate about fostering curiosity and purposeful relationships with the places we call home.

AleXeana harlem (elle/they/them) is a St. Louis-based artist, educator, herbalist, and cultural archivist. harlem creates "soft spaces for hard bodies" that combine fibers, photography, and textile with narratives of the land and its people. They use radical softness to bring hard selves back home, so that we may acknowledge the reality of our shared experiences to work toward a better existence. harlem studies cultural populations across the Americas to archive stories of people who may be misremembered. Their work explores themes of identity, culture, gender, queerness, memory keeping, and security. harlem is currently a Luminary Studio Resident and has exhibited at CAM St. Louis and throughout the United States.

Tosha Phonix is a food and nature enthusiast and entrepreneur dedicated to making healthy, fresh foods accessible and affordable for all. With a social service background, she strengthens urban growers' businesses through improved capacity and resource access. Since 2011, she has grown sustainable produce throughout St. Louis, taught chronically unhoused children to grow food, and founded an agriculture organization connecting local Black growers with rural farmers. As Co-Director of the Urban Farm at Muhammad Mosque and Founder and Executive Director of A.C.R.E.S. (Agriculture for Community Restoration, Economic Justice & Sustainability), Phonix continues to fight on behalf of food access within urban areas.

Rev. LaQuindlyn Shanae grew up between the Penrose and Academy neighborhoods. She dedicates this work to Mama Dora King, who molded the values she has today.

Ronda Smith Branch is a practitioner of liberatory well-being who discovered profound wisdom in the simple act of pulling up ivy from her historic home. Drawing from ancient African principles and the Bodhi seed tradition of enlightenment, she offers a unique perspective on personal transformation that honors both individual healing and collective liberation. Her approach weaves truth-telling, historical awareness, and natural healing into a practical philosophy for authentic living Ronda carries forward her mother's revolutionary legacy—

the gift of a voice that refuses to be silenced—while connecting to the long lineage of Black women who understood that speaking truth serves not just personal freedom but universal justice.

Frankie Williams is an artist and student. He graduated from Sumner High School, and some of his favorite memories and activities are hanging out in school and at CAM St. Louis with fellow *Field Guide* working group members, getting to know them and having a good time. In his art, he likes to paint, sketch, draw, and sew to make works that are dark, mindless, and macabre—but also cute. What he likes most about living in St. Louis, specifically The Ville neighborhood, is how safe it is. He likes seeing how city residents bring peace to one another and come together to build a community. In his spare time, he likes to relax and focus on personal projects and other programs.

Glossary

Ancestor: A person from whom one has descended.

Biomythography: A blend of autobiographical myth to express the complex reality of a person. This phrase was coined by Audre Lorde in *Zami: A New Spelling of My Name* (1982).

Ecology: The study of relationships and their environment.

Ecosystem: A community of living organisms.

Community: A social group with shared norms, identity, values, cultures, and interests.

Heal: To ease tension for the essence of who or what you are as a reality or form.

Native plants: Plants growing in an area prior to European settlement that have adapted to the soil and ecosystem for thousands of years.

Rematriation: "Indigenous women-led work that aims to restore sacred relationships between Indigenous people and ancestral land, honoring matrilineal societies," as defined by the Sogorea Te' Land Trust.

Seedbank: A place or group that stores seeds to preserve diversity for future generations.

Seedkeeping: The practice of collecting, drying, storing, and preserving seeds from plants, especially vegetables, grains, herbs, and flowers, for future planting and to ensure the continuation of specific heirloom varieties and open-pollinated seeds.

Common Native Plants

These plants are just a few that are native to North St. Louis and the surrounding area, and are also common to find and easy to maintain:

Aster (New England, purple, white)
Black cherry
Blue false indigo
Brown-eyed susan
Butterfly weed
Cardinal flower
Chokeberry
Coneflower / Echinacea
Eastern redbud
Evening primrose
Pawpaw tree
Prairie blazing star
Prairie dropseed
Sumac (fragrant, winged, smooth)
Sunflower
Wild plum

Image Credits

Cover: Fit and Food's *Rainbow Resilience Bed* (2025).
Photo: Alexis Creamer.

Page 13: Dail Chambers, *Untitled sketchbook artwork*, 2024–25.
Courtesy the artist.

Page 17: Map of St. Louis and "Common Fields," 1796.
Courtesy Missouri Historical Society.

Pages 24–25: Coahoma Orchards. Photo: Cary Brown.

Pages 26–27: Dail Chambers, *Untitled sketchbook artwork*, 2024–25. Courtesy the artist.

Page 31: Dail Chambers, *Saint Louis collage (red thread)*, n.d.
Courtesy the artist.

Pages 34–35: Photos: Dail Chambers.

Pages 36–37: Dail Chambers's sculpture *A River Journey* (2024) installed at CAM as part of the *Make the River Present* exhibition, on view March 7–August 10, 2025.
Photo: Izaiah Johnson.

Pages 38–44: Plant specimens collected by Dail Chambers in her sketchbook. Courtesy the artist.

Page 45: Dail Chambers, *Untitled sketchbook artwork*, 2024–25.
Courtesy the artist.

Pages 52–53: Coahoma Orchards. Photo: Cary Brown.

Page 50 (top): *The North St. Louis Creative Field Guide* working group visits Northside Workshop. Photo: Michelle Dezember.

Page 50 (bottom): Photo: Juan William Chávez.

Page 51: Bald eagle sighting at Northside Workshop.
Photo: Michelle Dezember.

Page 52 (top): Kiersten Torrez, Cary Brown, and Dail Chambers at Northside Workshop. Photo: Michelle Dezember.

Page 52 (bottom): Juan William Chávez at Northside Workshop.
Photo: Kiersten Torrez.

Page 53: Juan William Chávez and Dail Chambers plant a wild cherry tree sapling at Coahoma Orchards.
Photo: Michelle Dezember

Pages 56–57: Map of sites referenced in the *North St. Louis Creative Field Guide*. Courtesy WORK/PLAY.

Page 60: Juan William Chávez, *Charles Henry Turner: Garden as a Laboratory*, 2025. Citizen Scientist Zine. Courtesy the artist and Northside Workshop's Pollinator Press.

Page 61: Sumner High School students at "Growing Safe Spaces: Honoring Turner" workshop. Photo: Juan William Chávez.

Page 62: Instructions for creating a pollination apron.
Courtesy Juan William Chávez.

Page 63: Logo for "Growing Safe Spaces: Honoring Turner" workshop developed by LM Flowers and Sumner High School students, 2023.

Page 66: AleXeana harlem, *Our Ancestors' Compass Points North*, 2025. The work appeared in the *Access Is an Invitation: CAM Connect Showcase* exhibition, on view September 5, 2025–February 8, 2026. Photo: Izaiah Johnson.

Page 67: AleXeana harlem, *Dodier*, 2025. Courtesy the artist.

Pages 68–69: AleXeana harlem, *Neighborhood Circle*, 2025. Courtesy the artist.

Pages 73–75: Frankie Williams's *We're All Together* (2025) mural in progress. Photos: Michelle Dezember.

Page 78: Rev. LaQuindlyn Shanae. Photo: Michelle Dezember.

Pages 82–83: A depiction of John and Catharine O'Fallon's Athlone mansion and the surrounding grounds, which later became O'Fallon Park, from Richard J. Compton and Camille N. Dry's 1875 *Pictorial St. Louis* map. Courtesy Missouri Historical Society.

Pages 84–85: O'Fallon Park after the May 2025 tornado. Photos: Rev. LaQuindlyn Shanae.

Pages 90–91: Coahoma Orchards. Photos: Cary Brown.

Page 92: Cary Brown. Photo: Michelle Dezember.

Page 93: Coahoma Orchards. Photo: Cary Brown.

Page 97: Ronda Smith Branch. Photos: Tyler Small.

Pages 101–3: Gabi Cole at Fit and Food's *Rainbow Resilience Bed* (2025). Photos: Alexis Creamer.

Pages 107–9: *The North St. Louis Creative Field Guide* working group visits A.C.R.E.S. site in Walnut Park. Photos: Michelle Dezember.

Pages 116-19: Photos courtesy Alexis Creamer

Published on the occasion of the project *North St. Louis Creative Field Guide*, organized by the Contemporary Art Museum St. Louis.

Project Curator
Michelle Dezember

Community Engagement Lead
Alexis Creamer

Lead Artists
Dail Chambers, Juan William Chávez

Working Group Contributors
Cary Brown, Gabi Cole, AleXeana harlem, Tosha Phonix,
Rev. LaQuindlyn Shanae, Ronda Smith Branch, Frankie Williams

Editor
Graham Eng-Wilmot

Design
WORK/PLAY

Additional Photography
Izaiah Johnson, Tyler Small

Printing
Worth Higgins & Associates

ISBN: 979-8-90243-580-8

This project is supported in part by an award from the National Endowment for the Arts. Additional support is provided by the Regional Arts Commission of St. Louis.

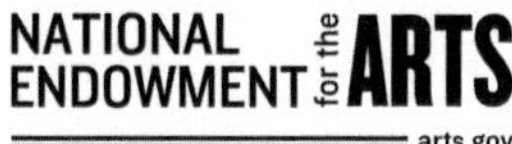

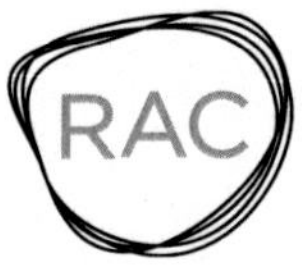

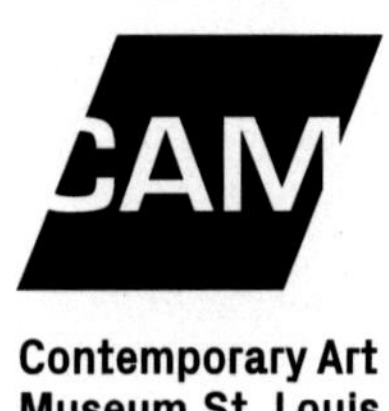
CAM
Contemporary Art
Museum St. Louis